S0-AYY-172

THE FLOATING CANADIAN DOLLAR

THE FLOATING CANADIAN DOLLAR

Exchange Flexibility and Monetary Independence

Paul Wonnacott

American Enterprise Institute for Public Policy Research
Washington, D. C.

Paul Wonnacott is professor of economics at the University of Maryland.

Foreign Affairs Study 5, May 1972

Library of Congress Catalog Card No. L.C. 72-82725

Printed in United States of America

CONTENTS

1
INTRODUCTION

Canada has had a flexible exchange rate for about half the period since the end of the Second World War—to be exact, from October 1950 until early 1962, and again since the beginning of June 1970. This Canadian experience represents the best modern evidence available on the working of a flexible exchange rate for a developed high-income country. Furthermore, because of the importance of the international sector to the Canadian economy, the flexible exchange rate plays a more important part in Canada's overall postwar economic history than it would otherwise. Of necessity, this history cannot be dealt with in anything approaching a complete manner in the present essay. Instead, the objectives here are (1) to highlight Canada's use of a flexible exchange rate as a method for dealing with disturbances in the country's international accounts and (2) to investigate the relationship between both the flexible and the fixed Canadian exchange rate and the development of aggregate demand policies aimed at achieving high employment and stable prices. The first two chapters outline some of the theoretical points in the exchange rate controversy, and the next three chapters discuss (1) Canadian experience during the early float of 1960-62, (2) the subsequent period of a pegged rate from 1962 to 1970, and (3) the recent float beginning June 1, 1970.[1] The sixth chapter investigates appropriate behavior for an exchange stabilization fund when the exchange rate is flexible. The concluding note summarizes the main findings of the study.

There are essentially four ways to adjust imbalances of international payments: (1) changes in relative domestic price levels, (2) changes in exchange rates, (3) changes in domestic real incomes, and

[1] The earlier experience is considered in much greater detail in my *Canadian Dollar, 1948-1962* (Toronto: University of Toronto, 1965).

(4) direct actions (such as tariffs or controls) to affect international transactions. Where imbalances are moderate, a fifth option may also be open: the financing of the imbalances in the hope or expectation that they will turn out to have been the result of transitory factors and will therefore disappear either of their own accord or with only mild and relatively costless corrective steps.

Adjustment through Exchange Rate Alterations

The argument for adjustment through exchange rate alterations is that this process provides a less costly response to payments imbalances than any of the alternatives. A country will be reluctant to restrict demand severely in the face of payments deficits because of the high level of unemployment which might result. Conversely, especially with the prevalence of inflation, a country will be unwilling to stoke up inflationary forces in the face of payments surpluses, and therefore may look to exchange appreciation as an alternative. Germany in 1961, 1969 and 1971, and Canada in 1950 and 1970, are examples. The appreciation may take the form of altering the official parity, as it did in Germany in 1961, or of abandoning the par for an indefinite period, as in Germany and the Netherlands in May 1971, and Canada in October 1950 and June 1970. An intermediate possibility is the temporary abandonment of a par to allow for a brief transitional period of floating prior to the reestablishment of a new par, as in Germany in the fall of 1969.

There is a spectrum of methods for altering exchange rates, running from sizable infrequent adjustments to completely free rates without government intervention. The many intermediate stages include frequent adjustments in par—which can be quite small and qualify as a "crawling peg" in the case of a country whose domestic rate of price change does not greatly differ from those abroad, or quite sizable and qualify as a "trotting peg," as in the case of Brazil.[2] During much of Canada's experience with exchange flexibility, particularly during the 1950s, the rate came quite close to a freely fluctuating one, in the sense that the government made

[2] The intermediate arrangements have been the subject of considerable study in recent years. See, e.g., International Monetary Fund, *The Role of Exchange Rates in the Adjustment of International Payments*, September 1970; Council of Economic Advisers, *Annual Report*, 1970, pp. 137-40; C. Fred Bergsten et al., *Approaches to Greater Flexibility of Exchange Rate: The Burgenstock Papers* (Princeton: Princeton University Press, 1970); and Juergen B. Donges, *Brazil's Trotting Peg* (Washington: American Enterprise Institute for Public Policy Research, 1971).

little or no attempt to get the exchange rate to correspond to any "target" value. At other times, however, the government attempted either to keep the exchange rate from changing in response to market conditions or to push it to a new level. Canada's efforts to affect the value of its currency—which were most notable at the beginning of the 1960s and again during the recent period of flexibility in 1970-71—are one of the major subjects considered in the chapters below.

In recent years, with the great increase in international capital mobility and, in particular, with the rapid development of the Euro-dollar market, international capital flows have commanded increasing attention both as a potential balance of payments disturbance and especially as an inhibition on independent monetary policies. The discussion of exchange flexibility has come to be dominated by the problem of monetary independence.

Indeed, monetary independence has become such a predominant theme in the discussion of exchange flexibility that the question may arise as to what happened to the older subject of exchange rate alterations as a method of adjusting payments imbalances. But this is to make an artificial distinction: if a balance of payments surplus cannot be adjusted through flexible exchange rates, strong pressures build up for monetary expansion within the country with the surplus—in other words, its monetary policies cease to be independent. The monetary complications of a fixed exchange rate provided a major impetus to the adoption of a flexible rate in Canada both in 1950 and in 1970. The theme of monetary independence through flexible exchange rates will be central in the chapters below. The theoretical highlights are given in Chapter 2, with the following Chapters 3 through 5 describing how problems arose in practice over the past two decades. The strong and unsurprising conclusion is that exchange rate adjustments can contribute significantly to independence of national monetary policies.

Exchange Rate Flexibility: Some Broader Considerations

If flexible exchange rates provide a degree of monetary independence, why then is there such reluctance to move toward such rates? The answer is that independence is not the only consideration. It may be bought at too high a price in terms of other competing goals (see the following section). Then too, the case for independence has been looked at from a national viewpoint, and it is important that the international system not degenerate to outright economic warfare. It was the desire to provide a break from the competitive nationalism of the thirties, when countries sought relief from unemployment by competitive devaluations, that the founders of the International Monetary Fund determined to make pegged exchange rates the basic standard of the postwar world. From a quantitative standpoint, the pursuit of national advantage at the expense of others (however that may be defined) has not been very important during the Canadian experiments with flexibility. However, potential problems of economic nationalism have played such an important part in the postwar determination to maintain pegged exchange rates that any study of flexible experiments would be incomplete without a consideration of this question (see Chapter 6). And it will gain importance as exchange flexibility becomes a more common phenomenon.

One further caveat is necessary with respect to the desirability of national policy independence. The case for freedom to follow independent demand policies is most clear if one country's leaders are more adept at responding to the needs of the economy than are the leaders of other countries. Thus, one of the arguments for flexible exchange rates is that they will allow a country to follow a course of stable prices in an inflating world. Yet, in the more general case, where economic policies are neither conspicuously good nor conspicuously bad, the case for independence is less certain. Each country is subject to its own particular disturbances. If policies are generally appropriate in reducing the effects of these disturbances, then independence is to be sought after. If, however, domestic authorities have only a mediocre ability to deal with disturbances, there is something to be said for being attached to the larger world economy through fixed exchange rates. As the overall world economy is subject to many and varying disturbances, any one disturbance tends to be diffused; being tied in with the average thus has the advantage of limiting the disturbing effects of any single shock to the domestic economy. But, whatever the failures of public policy, one would hope that the actions taken by the government are more likely to stabilize the economy than are the set of pressures arising from the external accounts. As a general proposition, institutional arrangements which increase the degree of national policy independence may be considered desirable.

Exchange Rate Flexibility: The Side Costs

Independence may, however, be bought at too high a price. For example, if exchange rate flexibility introduces a high degree of uncertainty into international trading and investment relationships, then the reduction in the level of international transactions might be so great as to offset the advantages of independence to be gained from exchange flexibility.

Uncertainties associated with exchange flexibility create a worrisome problem, and the standard reply by the advocates of exchange rate flexibility—that risks may be hedged in the forward market—is not altogether compelling, even in cases where there is a well developed and smoothly running forward market. Suppose, for example, that an importer contracts for a receipt of goods in three months time, and he is uncertain as to whether the domestic currency will stay steady, go up, or go down. He may cover in the foreign exchange market, thus assuring his ability to buy the imports at a fixed cost in terms of domestic currency. But suppose that his competitors do not cover and that the price of the home currency rises on the foreign exchanges. Then the competitor will be able to import at a cheaper rate than the merchant who covered. The merchant must either cover or not, and, whichever he does, he may be put at a disadvantage compared to his competitor if he has guessed wrong.

In this way, the possibility of exchange rate alterations introduces a risk into international trade which cannot be eliminated by forward market transactions. The relevant question in evaluating exchange rate flexibility, however, is not whether exchange risks exist and may inhibit the development of trade; rather, the relevant question is the comparative degree of these risks under flexible and pegged exchange rates.

No general answer can, of course, cover all possible cases. Nevertheless, the advocates of flexible exchange rates themselves have a convincing case against fixed rates. The system of pegged exchange rates does not guarantee exchange stability; there may be both the minor changes within the normal margins, and, more important, abrupt alterations in the exchange rate, such as took place in the United Kingdom in 1949 and 1967, France in 1969, and Germany in 1961 and 1969. Furthermore, the effort to protect the pegged exchange rate may lead to direct controls or other interference with trade and investment, such as the Canadian import surcharge of 1962-63 and the British surcharge of 1964-66. The uncertainties and disruptions to trade under a pegged exchange rate may exceed the uncertainties from exchange flexibility.[3]

[3] On the hedging of commercial transactions between the United States and Canada, see two papers prepared for the September 1971 Bald Peak conference

sponsored by the Federal Reserve Bank of Boston: Harry C. Eastman, "The Hedging of Commercial Transactions between U.S. and Canadian Residents," and Norman S. Fieleke, "The Hedging of Commercial Transactions between U.S. and Canadian Residents: A View from the United States." One of the interesting responses Fieleke received from the trading firms that he questioned came from a company concerned about possible sudden changes in the price of sterling. It hedged transactions in sterling, but said it would not hedge these transactions if the pound were allowed to float, since the risks associated with small changes would be acceptable (p. 12). Other respondents, however, declared preferences for fixed exchange rates, in part because of the arguments with customers over pricing following changes in the rate.

2

EXCHANGE RATES AND ECONOMIC INDEPENDENCE: THE INTERNATIONAL TRANSMISSION OF INFLATION

In recent years—in sharp contrast to the 1930s—inflation has become the major stabilization problem in the advanced economies. The transfer of inflationary pressures from one country to another may therefore now be used to illustrate the basic issues of economic interdependence. In practice, of course, it may not always be easy to identify the direction in which inflationary forces are being transmitted. Moreover, there is some natural tendency during a period of more or less general inflation for each country to blame every other country for causing the problem—with special nods being made in the direction of the U.S. because of the size of our economy, the central position of the U.S. dollar in international finance, and the propensity for American corporations to invest abroad.

Transmission of Inflation Under Fixed Exchange Rates

Current account: the price and volume of exports and imports. For illustration, suppose that, under a fixed exchange regime, powerful expansive forces emanate from a country. With strong domestic demand conditions, there will be a tendency for the country in question to import more and export less. In the economies of the trading partners, inflationary pressures will be created which may be looked at as having three aspects. First, where markets are closely linked across international borders, price increases in the original country may pull up prices of similar goods in the trading partner. Second, the increase in imports and decrease in exports in the original country will directly increase aggregate demand in the partner. Third, there may be an additional increase in aggregate demand if the central authorities acquire the foreign exchange (which they must buy in order to keep the exchange rate fixed) by simply expanding the money base, i.e., by buying the foreign exchange with newly created money.

Unfortunately, when one begins to dig into this threefold classification of the inflationary effects—(1) the direct (linked) effect on prices, (2) the direct effect on aggregate demand, and (3) the secondary effect on aggregate demand which may result from the monetization of the foreign exchange inflow—the distinctions among the three tend to become fuzzy. It is not clear, for example, that one should really distinguish the first, direct, effect on prices (#1) from the general increase in aggregate demand (#2). An increase of demand would seem to be integrally associated with an upward movement of prices, and to separate part of the increase in prices from the increase in demand would seem to be questionable. But there is a reason for this separation. In recent experience, in Canada and elsewhere, aggregate demand policy making has been greatly complicated by the stubborn tendency for prices to continue to rise after excess demand has been eliminated from the economy. At least in the short run a simple one-to-one relationship between demand and price changes can not be assumed; it is important to look at external disturbances to see their possible differential effects on prices and aggregate demand. This question of the possible direct impact of international prices on Canadian prices will be raised in the discussion of recent Canadian experience (below, Chapter 5).

In passing, it might be noted that, if one accepts the possibility that international prices may have an impact on domestic prices partially independent of their effect on the level of demand, there are grounds for considering inflationary forces emanating from the United States in the early sixties (when U.S. prices were reasonably stable in spite of the upward movement of demand) to have been different from those of the late sixties (when U.S. demand and prices were both moving up quite rapidly, and there was thus a double inflationary effect on other countries). There are also grounds for considering the inflationary forces of both periods to be different from the situation at the beginning of the seventies (when there was a continued upward movement of prices in spite of weakness in the economy).

Direct investment. In the capital accounts, the two major components may be distinguished: (1) direct equity investment, and (2) financial (debt) flows which respond primarily to interest rate and exchange rate incentives. This distinction, of course, is not the only way that capital flows may be divided; and, in particular, it slides over the distinction (made in the U.S. balance of payments accounts) between securities of less than one year to maturity (short-term) and those of more than one year. Apart from simplicity, the rationale for sliding over the one-year distinction is that there would seem to be little ground for distinguishing sharply the motives for acquiring debt securities according to the length to maturity. Motives for acquiring both short- and long-term debt include the acquisition of a higher interest rate than is available at home, the avoidance of an exchange loss (or the acquisition of an exchange gain in the event of an appreciation), and the avoidance of risk of default on the part of the issuing organization. In the discussion of the Canadian exchange rate, the distinction between securities on the basis of their maturity becomes particularly problematical. In fact, purchases of outstanding securities with more than one year to maturity have been a significant vehicle for speculation, particularly in the period immediately prior to the Canadian float in 1950.

If investment flows into a country, there will be an initial stimulative effect, the strength of which will depend in part on the degree to which the foreign direct investment represents "new" investment (as contrasted to the displacement of similar domestic investment which would otherwise have taken place) and on the stimulating effect of investments in one area on investments in related areas.

The effects of foreign direct investment on the total level of investment in Canada have been considered in some detail in the past decade. The issues are examined carefully in the work of Richard Caves of Harvard University and Grant Reuber of the University of Western Ontario.[1] They conclude that foreign investment does not act primarily to displace domestic investment, but that instead a dollar of direct foreign investment in Canada is generally associated with between $1.50 and $3.00 of Canadian capital formation spread more or less evenly over the three quarters following the direct investment inflow.[2]

---

[1] Richard E. Caves and Grant L. Reuber, *Capital Transfers and Economic Policy* (Cambridge: Harvard University Press, 1970); and a shorter version, *Canadian Economic Policy and the Impact of International Capital Flows* (Toronto: University of Toronto Press for the Private Planning Association of Canada, 1969), hereafter referred to as *Canadian Economic Policy.*

[2] *Canadian Economic Policy,* p. 34. For the view that foreign direct investment tends to discourage domestic Canadian investment, see Stephen Hymer, "Direct Foreign Investment and the National Economic Interest," in Peter Russell, ed., *Nationalism in Canada* (Toronto: McGraw-Hill, 1966).

In addition to the initial stimulation of demand, there may also be secondary effects because of the monetization of the balance of payments effects of the direct investment. Unfortunately, however, the direct investment case is more complicated than an increase in merchandise exports, because we cannot be certain whether the direct capital inflow will tend to be associated with a balance of payments surplus or deficit. Off the bat, the answer to this might seem to be obvious: in order for Americans or other foreigners to engage in direct investment in Canada, they will have to acquire Canadian dollars on the exchanges, and this will tend to add strength to the Canadian balance of payments. But suppose, for example, that a dollar of direct investment is associated with three dollars of total Canadian investment, and suppose that a high proportion of investment in Canada involves imports of machinery—say, one dollar in every three. In this case, there would be no tendency for direct investment to strengthen the balance of payments, and there would be no secondary stimulus arising from the monetization of the (actually nonexistent) foreign exchange inflow.

Once again, this question has been analyzed by Caves and Reuber, who found that, within a year's time horizon, it is uncertain whether direct capital flows will tend to cause a surplus or a deficit.[3] Without getting into the complications which this kind of analysis involves, it seems justifiable in the present discussion to push this secondary effect of the capital inflow to the back burner.

It should, however, be noted that Canada is somewhat unusual in this regard; indeed, the high Canadian propensity to import capital goods has long been noted as a strong force stabilizing the overall Canadian balance of payments in the face of large and variable capital movements. If one were to generalize the argument to include other countries, it is doubtful whether this secondary monetary impact of direct capital flows could be dismissed so readily. Indeed, one of the objections which has been made in Europe to American investment in that continent is that the investment contributes to inflationary pressure there. While it might justly be pointed out that these countries have their own share of homegrown inflation, it should be recognized that this objection is partly valid. So also is the related objection that, during periods of European balance of payments surpluses, the European central banks have in a sense been forced to finance American investment in Europe; that is, they have been forced to buy up the foreign exchange associated with the capital

[3] *Canadian Economic Policy,* pp. 40-41.

inflow in order to prevent the domestic currency from appreciating on the exchanges. One can take his choice, of course, as to whether the inflation in this case is attributable to the capital flows or to the fixed exchange rate, or both.

The stimulation of demand associated with foreign investment has been taken as an indicator of the contribution of investment to inflation during a period of overall high aggregate demand. While this concentration on the demand side follows the traditional discussion, and is generally satisfactory in evaluating short-run inflationary spurts, it becomes less satisfactory when a longer time horizon is considered. In the longer run foreign direct investment will not only contribute to the level of aggregate demand, but also add to the productivity of the economy and thus to the supply of goods. Hence, when one looks at an extended inflation—such as that from 1965 to 1969 in Canada—the contribution of foreign direct investment to total aggregate demand must be taken only as a qualified measure of the inflationary effect of the investment.

Portfolio investment. With fixed exchange rates and relatively mobile international capital, domestic interest rates are influenced by the level of foreign interest rates. An element of instability may therefore be introduced into the domestic economy.

Because of the cyclical behavior of interest rates, one cannot simply argue that inflation will be transferred in a steady and continuous manner from the inflating country via an interest rate mechanism to foreign countries. In the early stages of a cyclical upswing—such as in the United States in the early sixties—interest rates are likely to be relatively low, and there will be a tendency for portfolio capital to flow outward. This will stimulate the economies of foreign countries by keeping interest rates low and increasing the monetary base when the central authorities purchase the foreign exchange resulting from the capital inflow. (Alternatively, the authorities in the foreign countries may attempt to forestall the capital inflow by domestic open market purchases, which will have similar overall effects of downward pressures on interest rates and an increase in the reserve base.) Then as the expansion gains momentum and becomes inflationary, interest rates will tend to rise, first as a result of the demand for capital as investment opportunities improve, and later as a result of the tendency for both lenders and borrowers to discount nominal interest rates because of expected inflation (as in the United States in late 1965 and early 1966, and late 1967 and 1968). A final upward spurt in interest rates will come when strong monetary measures are taken to reduce the supply of loanable funds in an attempt to arrest the inflation (as in the U.S. in mid-1966 and 1969). Finally, when aggregate demand begins to show signs of weakening, there will be a tendency for interest rates to drop both because of the decline in investment demand and because of the easing of monetary policy in order to prevent a drastic downward swing in the economy (as in the U.S. starting in early 1970 and running into early 1971).

If foreign events are precisely synchronized with those at home, there will be no particular tendency for capital to flow. This is not likely to be the case. There will tend to be an outflow of capital in periods like the early and middle sixties, when the outflow led to the U.S. interest equalization tax and the voluntary and later mandatory foreign investment controls.[4] Again during the 1970-71 relaxation from very tight monetary conditions, there were international complications, including a flood of short-term capital flows into Germany which contributed to its decision to float in May 1971. (Although there were precipitating short-term capital flows prior to the Canadian float at the beginning of June 1970 [discussed in Chapter 5, below] and prior to the temporary German float of September-October 1969, there were strong trade forces at work in these two instances, and the May 1971 float of the Germans is the best illustration of the effects of swings in debt capital.) Similarly, there will be a tendency for the United States to attract financial flows during periods of very tight monetary conditions represented both by high interest rates and unavailability of funds, as in 1969. In this case the very large U.S. borrowings in Europe resulted in the reduction of European official holdings of dollars in 1969. Far from contributing to foreign inflation during that period, monetary conditions in the United States tended to exert an anti-inflationary pressure on Europe. Rather than simply look on capital flows from the United States—or any other country—as being solely a source of "inflation," therefore, it is best to look on such flows as being a potential source of disturbance which may operate in either direction. They may, of course, operate in a desirable direction. But they may not. In any case, with the growth of the Eurodollar market and the general increase in the mobility of capital, the magnitude of this potential source of disturbance has grown

[4] It might seem that the foreign direct investment controls should be put under the direct investment section rather than here. However, the FDI program was not designed to limit foreign direct investment as such, but rather to push the financing into foreign capital markets. Thus, the relative interest rates are a central consideration in the operation of the program.

rapidly. Because of the traditionally close financial connections between Canada and the New York capital market, the implications of a high degree of capital mobility came to the fore at an earlier stage in Canada than in Europe. Indeed, flows of portfolio assets across the border were a major contributor to the Canadian decision to allow the Canadian dollar to float in 1950 (see Chapter 3, below).

Means of gaining independence from international monetary disturbances. There are essentially five ways to deal with undesirable monetary consequences arising from the flow of debt capital across international boundaries. First, the flows may be (partially) controlled by direct actions taken either by the capital exporter (e.g., the U.S. interest equalization tax) or by the capital importer (e.g., German regulations forbidding the payment of interest on foreign-owned deposits). Second, exchange rates may be allowed to fluctuate, providing a degree of independence, as discussed in the next section, below. Third, it is possible for either the capital exporter or the capital importer or both to change the mixture of their policy in order to reduce the interest differential attracting the flow of capital. Low U.S. interest rates, for example, might be raised by a somewhat more expansive fiscal stance combined with a somewhat tighter monetary policy, leaving the overall trend of aggregate demand unchanged. In the capital recipients, the stress in anti-inflationary policies might be on the fiscal side, thus keeping interest rates relatively low. Fourth, if international capital flows are deemed to be much more responsive to short-term than long-term interest rates, an attempt might be made to discourage capital outflows from the United States by twisting the pattern of U.S. interest rates, pushing up short-term interest rates and pushing down long-term interest rates. Last, the capital exporter and importer may attempt to go more or less their own ways in domestic monetary policies, with arrangements being made to finance capital flows through recycling or other arrangements.

The borrowings of $3 billion by the Export-Import Bank and the United States Treasury in Europe in early 1971 may be considered a variation on this last possibility; they partially offset the effects of an outflow of private capital from the United States. Because of the position of the international dollar in the world economy, of course, the United States is in a somewhat different position from other countries regarding "recycling"; that is, its deficits may involve primarily the accumulation of dollars by foreign countries rather than the loss of reserve assets by the United States, and therefore the U.S. may have a degree of freedom in continuing capital exports without making arrangements to reacquire foreign exchange assets through recycling or other arrangements. This lies behind the European complaints of the United States ability to run "deficits without tears."

Each of the five methods has its advantages and disadvantages. Alterations in exchange rates are discussed separately in some detail below. Some of the problems with the other methods might be noted briefly.

Capital controls are cumbersome to administer, and it is difficult to make them effective without interfering with desirable international transactions. For example, a tight control on the flow of short-term capital will require regulations regarding the financing of exports and imports. Changes in the policy mix are cumbersome, and an attempt to tighten fiscal policy will run into difficult questions of how taxes are to be raised or expenditures pared. Needless to say, governments are likely to consider their freedom of maneuver here distinctly limited—as was the case in Canada in the fall of 1950, when exchange rate flexibility was chosen as the way out of the policy dilemma.

The exact extent of the ability of the central bank to "twist" the pattern of interest rates is a matter of controversy. Those on one side argue that long-term rates provide an unbiased predictor of future short-term rates [5] and that, therefore, the central bank does not have the power to change the pattern of the rates unless it chooses to change its overall height. On the other side, it is argued that the Federal Reserve can twist the rates, and should do so where required. Although this debate is far from settled, the power of the authorities to twist the rates is not of very great magnitude. Indeed, one of the interpretations of the rise in long-term interest rates in the United States in the second quarter of 1971 is that the authorities were trying to edge up short-term rates and that this foreshadowed a general increase in interest rates. (Another, and more weighty, argument is that doubts grew regarding the success of the anti-inflationary program, and that a continuing sizable allowance for inflation was therefore considered appropriate.) At any rate, the twist argument, whatever its strength,[6] is more applicable to U.S.-European capital flows

[5] David Meiselman, *The Term Structure of Interest Rates* (Englewood Cliffs, New Jersey: Prentice-Hall, 1962).

[6] Because interest costs increase when interest rate policy is used to attract capital flows, Thomas D. Willett and Francesco Forte argue (on the basis of a stock-adjustment model) that interest rate increases unaccompanied by general financial contraction will be ineffective in correcting balance of payments deficits. Willett and Forte, "Interest Rate Policy and External Balance," *Quarterly Journal of Economics*, May 1969, pp. 242-62.

than it is to U.S.-Canadian flows: the U.S. and Canadian capital markets are so closely associated at all maturities that capital flows can scarcely be considered isolated from the effects of changes in long-term interest rates. (As capital markets become increasingly integrated, the same is becoming true of U.S.-European interest rate relationships.)

The tentative attempts at recycling of the reserve changes resulting from capital flows in Europe in the late sixties provide little grounds for confidence in the general effectiveness of the recycling option, although there is some reason to believe that recycling can be both appropriate and effective if the only significant balance of payments disturbance is in the monetary capital accounts. The argument is that capital movements do not represent a "flow" of assets which will continue at a high rate as long as interest rate differentials exist; rather, they may more accurately be considered the reflection of the desire of asset-holders to readjust their portfolios. Thus, the opening of an interest rate differential will be followed by a relatively large movement of capital while asset-holders are readjusting their portfolios to the new situation, but as the readjustment takes place and the portfolios approach their new balance, the movement of capital will tail off. Ultimately capital movements will consist only of the movement attributable to the international allocation of new assets as the wealth of asset-holders grows. Furthermore, the elimination of the interest rate differentials should lead to a reversal of the capital flow.[7]

The apparent failure of recycling in Europe in the late 1960s did not so much throw doubt on the portfolio adjustment theory as indicate a general unease over fundamental exchange rate misalignments. Once reserves began to change rapidly, the question arose as to whether adjustments in exchange rates might be at hand. At this point, relative interest rates became a minor consideration compared to possible capital gains or losses following exchange rate adjustments, and the authorities found themselves in a poker game, with the speculators holding the high cards (the probability of a revalua-

---

[7] The portfolio adjustment theory may be found, e.g., in William H. Branson, *Financial Flows in the U.S. Balance of Payments* (Amsterdam: North-Holland, 1968); Herbert G. Grubel, "Internationally Diversified Portfolios," *American Economic Review*, December 1968, pp. 1299-1314; C. H. Lee, "A Stock Adjustment Analysis of Capital Movements: The United States-Canadian Case," *Journal of Political Economy*, August 1969, pp. 512-23; Norman C. Miller and Marina v. N. Whitman, "A Mean-Variance Analysis of United States Long-Term Portfolio Foreign Investment," *Quarterly Journal of Economics*, May 1970, pp. 175-96.

tion) and playing with cheap chips (since their losses would be limited to interest rate differentials, the costs of transactions, and perhaps a small exchange loss as the rate moved back towards the center of the official range) while the governments were putting real money on the line (i.e., the sizable capital losses on their reserves in the event of an exchange adjustment). In such a game, the wisdom of upping the stakes through recycling arrangements may be questioned. In this regard, it might be noted that one of the exponents of the portfolio adjustment theory, Professor Thomas Willett of Cornell University, has argued that the degree of exchange flexibility provided by a crawling peg will strengthen the case for recycling, since it will reduce the need for, and therefore the probability of, a jump in exchange rates.[8]

Exchange Flexibility and Economic Independence

While the effects of international disturbances may be desirable—as would be the case, for example, if there were an increase in the demand for a country's exports during a recession—there is no general assurance that this will be the case. Because of the limits of the alternative methods of providing a degree of independence noted above, exchange rate flexibility may be looked on as a promising method of attaining a degree of economic independence. The independence at issue here, it should be stressed, is an important, but narrowly defined, type of independence. It is the independence which comes from the ability to go one's own way so far as the overall level of demand in the domestic economy is concerned. It does not involve independence in the broader sense of isolation from the course of international economic events; the exporter of wheat, for example, is going to be adversely affected by a glut on the international wheat market regardless of the type of exchange rate mechanism in operation. The only way to get independence in the broader sense is to build a wall of tariffs and controls which choke off trade and investment.

Although the distinction cannot be made sharply, it is perhaps useful to divide the independence which comes from exchange rate flexibility into what may be called *passive* independence—the ten-

---

[8] Thomas D. Willett, Samuel I. Katz, and William Branson, *Exchange Rate Systems, Interest Rates, and Capital Flows* (Princeton Essays in International Finance, #78, January 1970), p. 4.

dency for the aggregate demand effects of outside disturbances to be neutralized as a result of market forces operating on the exchange rate—and *active* independence, an increased ability of the domestic authorities to implement aggregate demand policies, or an increased effectiveness of domestic policies resulting from exchange rate flexibility.

Passive independence. In the event of an increase in the foreign demand for the exports of a country, there will be both an initial stimulus arising directly from the export demand, and a secondary stimulus arising from the monetization of the reserve increase under a system of fixed exchange rates, as noted above. How will this be different if exchange rates are flexible?

In the event of a freely flexible exchange rate, there will be no acquisition of reserves by central authorities, and therefore the secondary stimulus will be absent. But this is not all. The initial strength of exports will tend to push up the price of the home currency, and thus discourage exports by raising their prices to foreign buyers and encourage imports by lowering their prices to domestic consumers. Assuming that neither the initial stimulus to exports nor the secondary effects resulting from the change in the exchange rate has any effect on fundamental capital flows, the outcome will tend towards a restoration of the previous trade balance. Additional exports of the products for which demand originally increased will be offset by decreases in other exports and increases in imports (although there may be time lags). The initial stimulus would eventually be neutralized.

In the case of an initial direct foreign investment, the outcome is less clear. If, for the moment, we accept Caves and Reuber's conclusion that, over the period of a year, there will be no notable tendency for direct investment inflows to cause a balance of payments surplus or deficit, then, over the year period the overall effect on the exchange rate should wash out—although there presumably would be an appreciation of the Canadian dollar initially (before the capital transfers have been "requited"), followed by a weakening of the rate. In contrast to the trade disturbance, the exchange rate effects should not be such as to offset the domestic stimulation arising from the initial inflow of direct investment; its net effect should still be stimulative in nature.

In the case of portfolio investment arising, let us say, from a reduction in foreign interest rates, the direct effect will be to lower interest rates and stimulate the domestic economy. It will, however, have an effect in raising the exchange value of the home currency, with the contrary tendency on aggregate demand. While exchange rate flexibility will tend to operate in the opposite direction to the effects of the lower interest rates, it is unclear whether the overall effects will be stimulative or deflationary. Caves and Reuber conclude on the basis of their empirical investigations that the net effects of portfolio capital inflows resulting from a decline in U.S. interest rates will stimulate the Canadian economy, while inflows owing to other outside disturbances are probably deflationary.[9] In the case of portfolio flows, as in that of external disturbances on the merchandise account, it is reasonable to argue that exchange rate flexibility provides a significant degree of passive independence. External disturbances do not greatly deflect the pattern of domestically-determined aggregate demand one way or another.

Active independence. The state of the balance of payments may inhibit the use of policies needed to reach the desired path of domestic aggregate demand. In the ultimate form of exchange flexibility—with no official intervention and no exchange rate "objective"—the state of the balance of payments ceases to act as a restraint on the adoption of policies, and active independence in this sense is achieved. In practice, authorities may have a balance of payments or an exchange rate target even with exchange flexibility; this clearly can be deduced from official statements in Canada in the past year [below, Chapter 5]. In this case, flexibility of exchange rates provides a degree of freedom in the adoption of policies, but it is clearly no longer a yes-or-no question. The more interesting question is what exchange rate flexibility does to the *effectiveness* of policies.

1. *Monetary policy.* An expansive monetary policy, by stimulating aggregate demand, will tend to increase the demand for imports, thereby causing a depreciation in the price of the home currency and encouraging exports. Thus, exchange rate flexibility will stop foreign "leakages" in demand and contribute to the domestic effects of the monetary policy.

Given some degree of international capital mobility, there is also another channel through which monetary policy operates. As interest rates begin to fall as a result of the expansive monetary policies, capital will begin to flow abroad, causing a depreciation in the home currency, and stimulating the economy because of the resultant sub-

[9] Caves and Reuber, *Canadian Economic Policy*, p. 43.

stitution of domestic products for imports and because of the increase in exports. Thus, a second and potentially powerful channel of operation of monetary policy will be opened up by exchange rate flexibility. Indeed, if capital mobility is very high, this international channel may become the most important channel through which monetary policy operates.

It is indeed sometimes argued that, with perfect capital mobility, the domestic channel for monetary policy will be completely closed off, and the *only* effects of monetary policy will come through the changes in the exchange rate. The argument here—that domestic interest rates cannot change and therefore monetary policy cannot work domestically if capital is perfectly mobile—also involves the assumption of a unitary elasticity of expectations with respect to the exchange rate. (That is, people firmly expect the exchange rate to remain at its most recent quotation, regardless of how much it may have changed in the recent past.) Quite apart from the interesting question of whether monetary policy may affect aggregate demand through channels other than changes in the nominal rates of interest, I cannot accept this argument in its extreme form. The unitary elasticity of expectations assumption involves a logical contradiction when combined with the assumption of perfect capital mobility. Suppose that we make these two assumptions; and suppose, also, that at 12:00 noon on January 2, the Bank of Canada puts in a bid for $100 million in securities on the open market. The "perfect markets" theory suggests that the total $100 million will flow abroad, leaving no effect on Canadian interest rates. The Canadian dollar will then fall. But the question then becomes, by how much? The theoretical answer is, by whatever is necessary to "balance" the international accounts, that is, by whatever is necessary to increase the Canadian trade balance by $100 million. How much is that, in the hour between 12:00 noon and 1:00 p.m.? There is *no* exchange rate which can affect the trade account to this degree and with this speed. What then must happen? As the Canadian dollar falls, the question must sooner or later be asked whether it is not in some sense "too low," i.e., lower than it is likely to be in the future. The moment the answer to that question becomes yes, equilibrium Canadian interest rates become lower than those abroad; the holder of Canadian securities is compensated for the lower interest rates by the expected exchange appreciation. The internal contradiction disappears when we discard the assumption of a unitary elasticity of expectations with respect to the exchange rate. In this case, however, domestic interest rates can be depressed by open market purchases even if capital is perfectly mobile; monetary policy still has a domestic channel through which to operate.[10]

2. *Fiscal policy*. If capital flows are for the moment ignored, the effectiveness of fiscal policy is also augmented by a flexible exchange rate. As the economy expands and imports tend to rise, the exchange rate will fall and there will be a stimulating effect on the export industries. Once again, as for monetary policy, the effectiveness of fiscal policy will be increased by the tendency for the currency to depreciate and eliminate external leakages of demand.

If the possibility of a high degree of capital mobility is introduced, the situation is less clear. If we skip over the question of whether government spending financed through the central bank should be considered "monetary" or "fiscal" policy, and assume simply that the government spending is financed by the sale of bonds to the public, the fiscal expansion should lead to upward pressures on the rate of interest. This would attract capital, and tend to put upward pressure on the price of the home currency on the international exchanges.

There will thus be two contrary pressures on the exchange rate—an upward pressure arising from the capital flow, and a downward pressure resulting from the tendency for imports to rise as a result of the fiscal stimulus. Which way the exchange rate will tend to go in the face of these conflicting pressures is uncertain. There will be a greater tendency for the home currency to depreciate—and therefore for exchange flexibility to contribute to the effectiveness of fiscal policy in stimulating demand—the greater the direct stimulative effect

[10] For the seminal article on capital flows and stabilization policy, in which are found the twin assumptions of perfect capital mobility (meaning that "a country cannot maintain an interest rate different from the general level prevailing abroad") and unitary elasticity of expectations regarding the exchange rate, see Robert A. Mundell, "Capital Mobility and Stabilization Policy under Fixed and Flexible Exchange Rates," *Canadian Journal of Economics and Political Science*, November 1963, pp. 475-85 (hereafter cited as Mundell, "Capital Mobility"). Mundell notes that these assumptions involve an overstatement of his case. Other important contributions to the extensive literature on capital mobility and stabilization policy include: William Fellner et al., *Maintaining and Restoring Balance in International Payments* (Princeton University Press, 1966); J. M. Fleming, "Domestic Financial Policies under Fixed and under Floating Exchange Rates," *IMF Staff Papers*, November 1962, pp. 369-79; Anne O. Krueger, "The Impact of Alternative Government Policies under Varying Exchange Systems," *Quarterly Journal of Economics*, May 1965, pp. 195-209; R. A. Mundell, "The Appropriate Use of Monetary and Fiscal Policy for Internal and External Stability," *IMF Staff Papers*, March 1962, pp. 70-77; and R. A. Mundell and A. K. Swoboda, eds., *Monetary Problems of the International Economy* (Chicago: University of Chicago Press, 1968).

of fiscal policy on the economy, the greater the marginal propensity to import, the greater the tendency for fiscal expansion to be financed through the central bank, and the lower the mobility of capital.[11] Empirical evidence in the Canadian case suggests that, if we eliminate any tendency for the central bank to finance government deficits, then the probable effects of expansive fiscal policy under flexible exchange rates is an appreciation of the Canadian dollar, at least in the short run.[12] The capital inflow effects outweigh the current account effects of higher imports; the exchange value of the currency rises; and the effectiveness of the fiscal policy is reduced.

In summary, then, exchange rate flexibility adds to the effectiveness of monetary policy as a stabilization tool. It may operate either way on the effectiveness of fiscal policy, although the evidence is that, in a country such as Canada, with a close connection to international capital markets, exchange rate flexibility probably dulls effectiveness of fiscal policy in the short run.

Looking at the question somewhat differently, it may be seen that capital mobility increases the effectiveness of monetary policy under flexible exchange rates (in contrast to its dulling effect on monetary policy under fixed exchange rates), and diminishes the effectiveness of fiscal policy under flexible exchange rates (in contrast to its contribution to the effectiveness of fiscal policy under fixed exchange rates). The reason for the contrast between fixed and flexible rates in this regard is relatively straightforward. Strength in the balance of payments under a fixed exchange rate results in an inflow of reserves, with expansive effects on the monetary system and therefore on the economy as a whole. Under flexible exchange rates, balance of payments strength results in an appreciation of the currency, and therefore in restraining effects on exports and import-substitutes.

---

[11] Again, a limiting case has been put forward, that fiscal policy will *completely* lose its effectiveness in the event of *perfect* capital mobility. See Mundell, "Capital Mobility," p. 484. Again, I cannot accept the validity of this limiting case. It requires, among other things, the assumption that income cannot change as a result of fiscal policy unless either the money supply changes or interest rates change.

[12] Rudolf R. Rhomberg, "A Model of the Canadian Economy under Fixed and Fluctuating Exchange Rates," *Journal of Political Economy*, February 1964, pp. 1-31; Caves and Reuber, *Canadian Economic Policy*, pp. 51-52, and 63-66. This conclusion is based on data from the earlier period of Canadian exchange flexibility in 1950-62.

3
THE EARLY FLOAT, 1950-62

The first seventeen years of the postwar Canadian exchange rate experience can be broken down into three periods, each containing its lesson regarding the relationship between exchange rates and domestic economic policies. During the early postwar period, from the end of the war until 1950, an attempt was made to operate an adjustable peg system. While the importance of the exchange rate to performance of the domestic economy was specifically recognized—especially in the 1946 decision to use an appreciation of the Canadian dollar as a means of lessening postwar inflationary pressures—the experience cannot be regarded as a happy one. In particular, the rapidly changing cross-currents in the international economy made it very difficult to choose a pegged rate in which confidence could be placed. The exchange value of the Canadian dollar was raised in 1946, lowered in 1949, and in 1950 there were strong upward market pressures which made the value chosen in 1949 untenable. The inability to choose an appropriate lasting rate was the reason for the initial decision to abandon a pegged rate in favor of flexibility in 1950.

During the second period—running from 1950 to about 1958—the flexibility of the exchange rate provided an automatic adjustment to external changes, particularly in 1951-52, when strength of Canadian exports led to a rise of about 10 percent in the exchange value of the Canadian dollar. Because of the flexibility of the exchange rate, Canada avoided the monetary complications which otherwise would have arisen from an external surplus at a time of excess domestic demand. This period illustrated the value of a flexible exchange rate in providing the "passive independence" discussed in Chapter 2. Canada followed roughly similar policies to those pursued in the United States, in response to roughly similar domestic conditions;

the shifts in external payments did not noticeably deflect Canadian policies.

During the third period—from about 1958 to the repegging of the Canadian dollar in 1962—there was a divergence between Canadian and United States monetary conditions. Canada pursued "active independence" during much of this time in the form of tighter monetary policies, which showed up most obviously in the form of wider spreads between Canadian and U.S. interest rates. The strains caused by these tight monetary policies during a period of high unemployment, and the complications arising from a high exchange value of the Canadian dollar, led to a sharp policy reaction in the early sixties, and to a repegging of the dollar in May of 1962. Something clearly went wrong during this period, but the evidence points more to incorrect policies than to any fundamental defect in the flexible exchange rate system itself.

Prelude to the Float: 1946-50

When Canada entered the Second World War with Britain in September of 1939, the Canadian dollar was devalued to 90.9¢ (U.S.) from the approximate par at which it had been trading since 1933. At the same time, extensive foreign exchange control was instituted to conserve scarce foreign exchange for use in the war effort.

In the middle of 1946, the Canadian government decided to repeg the dollar at par with its U.S. counterpart. The major reason for this decision was not the strength of the Canadian balance of payments, but rather the strong inflationary pressures and the contribution which a higher value of the Canadian dollar could make to lessening these pressures.[1] Because of the widespread skepticism at that time regarding the effectiveness of monetary policy, the government was interested in other ways to reduce inflation: the appreciation of the currency promised some help in this regard. In spite of the inflationary pressures, monetary conditions at this time remained very conducive to expansion. Long-term interest rates declined between November 1945 and March 1946 from 2.95 percent to 2.55 percent, where they remained through the rest of 1946 and 1947.

During 1945 and early 1946, there had been a considerable buildup of Canadian reserves of gold and U.S. dollars (from about

---

[1] Douglas Abbott, Minister of Finance, *Debates, House of Commons,* July 5, 1946. For greater detail on the pre-1962 Canadian experience, see my *Canadian Dollar, 1948-1962* (Toronto: University Press, 1965), and the references therein.

$900 million to about $1,600 million). A slight decline had begun prior to the revaluation, and, in the following sixteen months, the decline became very steep, with total losses amounting to $1 billion by late 1947. The government responded with a series of controls, including prohibitions on the importation of a number of goods, and a restoration of travel restrictions similar to those imposed during the war. Excise taxes were imposed on consumer durables in order to discourage imports from the United States. Although some of the controls lingered on into 1950, they lasted in their severe form only through 1948.

The losses of dollar and gold reserves, which precipitated the controls, were not so much a result of weakness in the overall payments position of Canada as of the triangular nature of Canadian payments. While Canada had an overall surplus on current account during 1947, it had a deficit of over $1.1 billion with the United States on current account, and there was a net repatriation of over $200 million of long-term capital to the United States. Because of the "dollar shortage" of the European countries, Canada received inadequate U.S. dollar payments from its surplus with Europe to cover its U.S. deficit. The initiation of the Marshall Plan in 1948 thus played a major part in the easing of the Canadian reserve problem, by making U.S. dollars available to Europe for the financing of imports, including over $450 million in imports from Canada by the end of 1948. The 1947-48 exchange crisis was not so much a sign that the external value of the Canadian dollar was inappropriate as the result of a fundamental imbalance between Europe and the United States.

For about a year following the imposition of the Canadian controls, the Canadian current account with the United States strengthened, with an atypical bilateral surplus being registered in the third quarter of 1948. This was accompanied by a recovery of about half a billion dollars in reserves of gold and U.S. dollars, with the $1 billion level again being reached in early 1949. Thereafter, however, reserves leveled out, and the current account balance showed some signs of weakening. When the British devalued in September of 1949, Canada responded defensively by lowering the value of her currency back to 90.9¢ (U.S.). This followed the historical pattern: during the interwar period, movements in the Canadian dollar vis-à-vis the U.S. dollar had closely followed the pattern of the pound, with the Canadian changes being about half the amplitude of the British.

While the historical intermediate position of the Canadian dollar between the U.S. dollar and the pound made the Canadian devaluation in September of 1949 seem like a reasonable defensive move, it was soon followed by a strong upward trend in Canadian reserves. The current balance showed little sign of strength and in fact became weaker after the currency realignments; but the capital accounts became very strong with the American direct investments following the discovery of oil in the Canadian West. By early June, 1950—that is, before the outbreak of the Korean War—speculation was appearing in the press that a revaluation was in the works. Weight was added to these rumors by an unguarded statement by a cabinet minister (C. D. Howe):

> It is true, at the moment, that Canadian funds are at a 10 percent discount, but that is a temporary situation. The historic position of the Canadian dollar is at par with the United States. How long that discount will continue I don't know . . . but it may not continue for very long.[2]

One of the standard arguments made against the adjustable peg system is that it requires government officials to insist on the validity of existing exchange rates, irrespective of their actual views regarding the fundamental situation. Howe's statement in 1950, a somewhat similar dissent from the existing rate of 92½¢ by the Canadian minister of agriculture in June of 1962, and the openness with which the appropriateness of the exchange rate was debated in Germany prior to the 1969 revaluation all show that officials do not always live up to this expectation.

With the outbreak of the Korean War, a major new complication was introduced. While there was still some hesitation in the use of monetary restraint as a means of containing inflation—the discount rate was not raised from its extremely low wartime level of 1½ percent until mid-October, 1959—skepticism regarding its effectiveness had been wearing away, and in the late summer the Bank of Canada engaged in open market sales of securities in order to offset the inflationary effects of the Korean War and of the large inflow of capital from the United States. By exerting an upward pressure on Canadian interest rates, these open market sales slowed the narrowing of interest rate differentials between Canadian and U.S., and hence tended to offset any dampening effects which a relative reduction in Canadian interest rates might have had on the inflow of capital from the United States. Thus, the normal market mechanism limiting capital inflows—the tendency of capital inflows to reduce interest rates and therefore reduce the incentive to purchase additional secu-

[2] As quoted by the *Financial Post* (Toronto), June 10, 1950, p. 1.

rities—was being interrupted by the Bank of Canada for domestic stabilization reasons. The capital inflow continued unabated, and, as questions increasingly arose regarding the tenability of the 90.9¢ peg, the flow became a veritable flood. During the third quarter of 1950, there was a short-term capital inflow of more than $600 million (Canadian), with much of this being concentrated in late September. (To give an idea of relative magnitudes, Canadian GNP in 1950 was $18.0 billion.)

Something clearly had to be done to deal with the capital inflow, and with the disruptive effects it was having on domestic monetary conditions. An upward revaluation of the currency would have been a possibility, but there had already been two rate adjustments since the war, and the government felt little confidence that any new rate would be appropriate over an extended period. Exchange flexibility was chosen as the way out of the dilemma.

The Early and Middle Fifties

For about the first eight years of the float, until the late fifties, the flexible exchange rate provided a relatively smooth method of adjustment to external changes. The greatest of these took place between June 1951 and September 1952, when there was a strong upward movement of the Canadian dollar from 93.5¢ to 104.2¢. In the year from mid-1951 to mid-1952, the Canadian merchandise balance was much stronger than in the preceding twelve months, swinging from a deficit of $388 million to a surplus of $484 million. Almost all of this swing was with countries other than the United States, where Canada was making large purchases of capital goods, and where the improvement amounted to only $93 million. (The tendency for Canada to import capital goods from the United States has been an important factor in the stability of the Canadian balance of payments, with monetary capital inflows and imports of capital equipment tending to offset one another in the balance of payments.) Wheat exports to Europe were particularly strong, rising from $135 million to $200 million to the United Kingdom, and from $60 million to $145 million to the continent.

During the rest of the fifties, the range of fluctuation of the Canadian dollar was relatively small—between 99.9¢ and $1.062. This stability was due primarily to underlying conditions, and not to official intervention by the Exchange Fund Account. Intervention was limited (averaging less than $20 million per month), and, in any case,

Figure 1

THE CANADIAN DOLLAR IN TERMS OF THE UNITED STATES DOLLAR
1950-1962

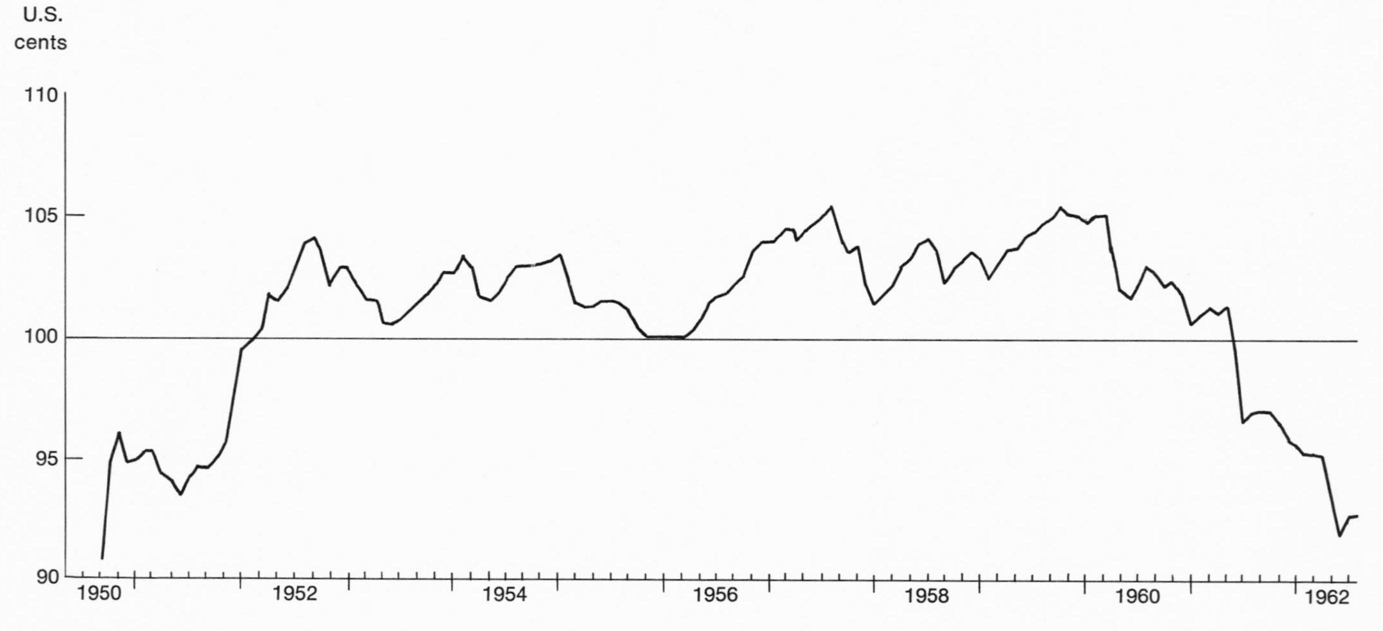

Source: Federal Reserve Bulletin.

it was not designed to counteract the longer and larger adjustments in the exchange rate: the fund followed a strategy of intervening to smooth out short-run changes, but tended to withdraw from the market in the face of persistent one-way movements of the rate.

In practice, the Canadian exchange situation after 1951 was quite close to what it would have been if there had been a pegged rate of $1.03, and margin of 3 percent on either side of this peg. This is, of course, very much an *ex post* judgment, and it is difficult to see how such an "equilibrium" rate could have been anticipated at the beginning of 1952. The point, however, is that the rate was very stable, and there was no evidence of the low elasticities and highly perverse short-term capital movements which, it is sometimes feared, will make a flexible exchange rate highly unstable. Indeed, short-term capital movements were of a stabilizing character: those involved in short-term capital transactions across the Canadian border acted as if they expected swings in the flexible rate to be reversed.[3]

Several points stand out regarding the relationship between monetary independence and the flexible exchange rate during this 1950-58 period. The adoption of flexibility in the fall of 1950 provided relief from the bind created for Canadian monetary policy by the inflow of short-term capital, and the desire for a degree of independence from international complications was a major reason for the initial decision to allow the rate to float. A year later, with the strong upward movement in the Canadian dollar in 1951-52, the float provided an escape mechanism from the inflationary pressures which would otherwise have accompanied payments surpluses. During the middle fifties, the importance of exchange flexibility was diminished, since the basic stability of the rate decreased the importance of having a "safety valve" for balance of payments pressures. There was, however, one period—from mid-1956 to mid-1957—when Canadian interest rates rose relative to those in the United States, and the simultaneous increase of about 5 percent in the exchange value of the Canadian dollar facilitated this anti-inflationary policy. This movement was in line with domestic needs: during 1956, Canadian prices rose more rapidly than those in the United States, and the unemployment rate was low during 1956 and early 1957 (although it did begin to move upward rapidly in the middle of 1957).

---

[3] Richard E. Caves and Grant L. Reuber, *Capital Transfers and Economic Policy: Canada 1951-62* (Cambridge: Harvard University Press, 1971), pp. 73-79; hereafter cited as Caves and Reuber, *Capital Transfers.*

The Twilight of the Flexible Rate: 1958-62

While the flexible exchange rate can be considered to have moved in a way which, on the whole, eased domestic problems prior to 1958, it became a source of discontent at the end of the fifties and during 1960 and 1961. From the end of the war until late 1957, the (seasonally adjusted) unemployment rate had been consistently below 5 percent, but during 1958-61 it averaged 6.8 percent, and never fell below 5.5 percent. The exchange value of the Canadian dollar rose to 105.75¢ in late 1959, and remained above par with the U.S. dollar until the 1961 budget speech, when Finance Minister Donald Fleming declared the government's intention to push it down. This high rate of exchange was associated with continuing large current account deficits (averaging over $1.2 billion in 1959-61), which were naturally resented at a time of high unemployment.

Something was clearly wrong in the Canadian economy, but it is difficult to attribute the problems to the flexible exchange rate mechanism itself. Instead, the problem was inappropriately tight monetary policies. Not only did these tight monetary policies have a direct restraining effect on the economy, but by attracting capital and pushing up the exchange value of the Canadian dollar, they also had a particular depressing effect on export and import-competing industries. The economic system worked much as theory suggests it should have, with capital inflows and an appreciation of the Canadian dollar providing an international mechanism through which the restrictive effects of tight monetary policies were increased. The puzzle lies in the monetary policies pursued in those years.

The start of monetary tightness is often traced to the Conversion Loan of 1958, although the effects of that operation were hidden in the short run by the efforts of the Bank of Canada to keep stable conditions in the bond markets while the loan was digested. In early 1958, the government became increasingly concerned with congestion in the Canadian bond markets and with the overhang of large wartime loans which were approaching maturity. It therefore announced a major program to refinance the government debt in July of 1958, and during the next two months, a total of no less than $5,800 million, or 37 percent of outstanding federal debt, was retired in exchange for bonds with longer maturities. To ensure the stability of bond prices during the conversion, the Bank of Canada supported the market, increasing its holdings of longer term securities by over $400 million between July and September. Much of the immediate monetary effect was offset by a decline of over $300 million in short-term government holdings of the bank.

There was a clear desire on the part of the government to use the Conversion Loan as a means for alleviating technical problems associated with the overhang of issues approaching maturity, but the relationship between the loan and overall economic strategy was less clear. The loan was defended both as an anti-inflationary step, and as a method for stimulating immediate expansion. Fuzziness regarding overall objectives was perhaps understandable in the light of continuing inflation during a period of high unemployment (7 percent in mid-1958), and of a growing tension over monetary policy between Finance Minister Donald Fleming and Bank of Canada Governor James Coyne.

During 1959 and 1960, any ambiguity was cleared up: monetary policy became and remained unquestionably tight. Between the last quarter of 1958 and the last quarter of 1959, the money supply actually decreased, and in the last quarter of 1960 it was either the same as in the last quarter of 1958, or only 3.5 percent greater, depending on whether personal savings deposits are included in the money supply or not. Interest rate differentials between Canada and the United States shot up in the last half of 1959, particularly those on government securities. Provinces and municipalities were increasingly driven to the New York capital market. In late 1959, the Canadian dollar rose to 105.75¢ U.S. During 1959, the current account deficit hit a peak of $1.5 billion.

Such tight monetary conditions scarcely seemed appropriate to conditions in the economy: the price level was relatively stable (with consumer prices rising less than 1.5 percent per annum in 1959 and 1960), while unemployment rose steadily in late 1959 and through 1960 to reach a rate of 7.6 percent in the last quarter of 1960 (seasonally adjusted). Why a tight money policy was followed during this period is hard to understand. Certainly the governor of the Bank of Canada was preoccupied with the danger of inflation,[4] and his statements regarding the international economy indicated some confusion. In his *Annual Report*, 1959, he argued:

> For some years, as I see it, the Canadian economy has been under the influence of excessive overall spending, which even in periods of relatively high unemployment resulted in a net inflow of imports from other countries. Attempts to induce growth for a short time at rates which in the aggre-

[4] See, for example, Bank of Canada, *Annual Report*, 1958, pp. 9-10.

Figure 2
CANADIAN - U.S. YIELD DIFFERENTIALS
1951-1962

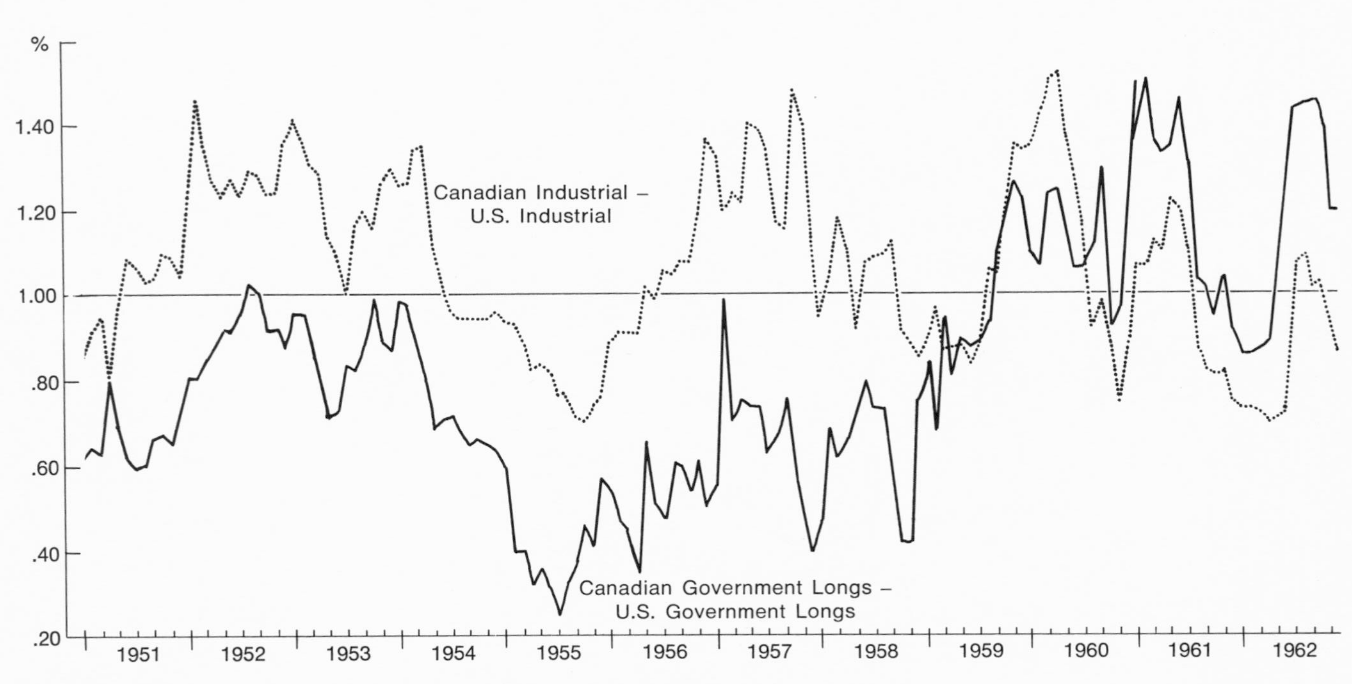

Source: *Bank of Canada Statistical Summary; Federal Reserve Bulletin.*

gate cannot be expected to continue, bring set-backs and unemployment in their train. Such conditions of excessive demand create inflationary pressures. . . .[5]

But it makes little sense to look on a merchandise deficit as an indicator of excess demand and inflationary pressures, without regard to the level of unemployment and the rate of price change. Furthermore, with a flexible exchange rate, this line of argument is an invitation to disaster. If a current deficit is taken as evidence of inflationary pressures, irrespective of the level of unemployment, and if tighter money is considered the proper response to inflationary pressures, then policy becomes essentially unstable. A tight policy, with higher interest rates, will cause an inflow of capital and an upward movement of the exchange value of the Canadian dollar; this will cause a deterioration of the current account; this will be taken as evidence of more inflation; in turn, this will be taken as indicating the need for yet tighter policies.

Tighter monetary policies under a flexible exchange rate operate as a restraint on the economy both because of the direct domestic effects of higher interest rates as a deterrent to investment, and because of capital inflows and the resulting depressing effects of the currency appreciation on the merchandise accounts. Nevertheless, one cannot categorically conclude that the capital flows themselves are deflationary, since the capital flows add to the supply of funds available for domestic investment, and therefore act to offset the direct domestic effects of tighter money. Much depends on the assumptions regarding monetary conditions in the absence of the capital flows. If one looks simply at the effects of portfolio capital flows on Canadian investment, on the one hand, and on the exchange rate and the current balance, on the other, then empirical evidence does not give a clear indication as to whether the overall effects are likely to be inflationary or deflationary.[6] If, however, monetary policy is set in such a manner as to have a specific restrictive effect on domestic investment, then by assumption the monetary authorities respond to offset the domestic investment effects of the capital flow, and it is therefore on balance deflationary. If an even stronger assumption is made, that monetary authorities respond to the capital inflow and the consequent current deficit by further tightening of monetary policy—as seems to be suggested by the quotation from the Bank of Canada's *Annual Report*—

[5] Ibid., p. 7.

[6] Caves and Reuber, *Capital Transfers*, pp. 288-93, especially page 292.

then the capital inflow becomes *highly* restrictive. The critical question is not the capital flow itself, but rather the basis on which monetary policy is made.

The resignation of the governor of the Bank of Canada. Because of tight monetary conditions, there were growing criticisms of the governor of the Bank of Canada. As early as March of 1958, there was a public squabble between him and Finance Minister Donald Fleming, who disagreed with his contention that monetary policy had not been tight. The dispute grew out of the charges during the election campaign that the bank was responsible for depressed economic conditions, and out of the governor's attempts to defend his record in his *Annual Report* for 1957. In the course of his defense, the governor depended on an overly narrow definition of tight money:

> . . . the impression seems to have arisen that the money supply was actually being contracted. This was not the case. The supply of money increased and its velocity of circulation rose very substantially. The phrase "tight money policy" may sometimes be used to refer to matters other than monetary matters, such as policy with regard to government taxation, expenditure and lending. To the extent that the phrase might be taken to imply a contraction in the availability of money it is not applicable. In this sense of the phrase there has never been a "tight money policy" since the establishment of the central bank twenty-three years ago.[7]

In an economy in which productive capacity is growing, an actual decline in monetary aggregates might be taken as an indicator that money is more than simply "tight." It might rather be an indication that monetary policy was *very* tight.

Much of this particular dispute applied to the period of 1956 and the first half of 1957, when a considerable degree of monetary tightness was appropriate because of the buoyancy of the Canadian economy. The dispute over the concept of monetary tightness did not, therefore, shed direct light on the question which should presumably be at the center of any discussion of monetary policy—the appropriateness of monetary policy as a means of achieving price, employment, and other goals. The dispute was, however, important as an indication of the hard line which the governor took on monetary policy, and the strong distaste of the finance minister for his hard

[7] Bank of Canada, *Annual Report*, 1957, p. 15.

line.[8] It dramatized the growing tenseness of the relationship between the minister and the governor, and foreshadowed the explosion which was yet to come.

The bank's *Annual Report*, 1957 also drew fire from the academic community. In a paper delivered to the Canadian Political Science Association in Edmonton in June of 1958, H. S. Gordon and L. M. Read of Carleton University (Ottawa) attacked the procedures of the governor in presenting his case that monetary policy had not been tight. "The expansion of the money supply, as presented by the 1957 *Annual Report*," they argued, "is inflated by the choice of definition and exaggerated by the method of measurement." [9] Their judgment of the recent reports of the bank was harsh:

> an overriding objective of these reports, it would appear, is to disarm public critics even at the expense of minimization, on the one hand, of the Bank's role in unpopular developments and exaggeration, on the other hand, of the Bank's role in popular ones. Even statistical data have been subserved to this objective. The reports, in consequence, contain casuistic, ambiguous, and misleading argument to a provocative degree.[10]

As monetary conditions became tighter and less appropriate with the upward movement of the unemployment rate, dissatisfaction with the policies of the Bank of Canada grew. In the late summer of 1959, the minister of finance was known to be particularly unhappy with the bank because of the treasury bill tender rate in excess of 6 percent. The policies of the bank and the speeches of the governor increasingly led university economists to question his competence, and in 1960 twenty-nine of them signed a letter to the minister of finance asking that steps be taken "to alter the management of the Bank of Canada." [11]

In spite of the widespread differences with the governor's policies, both within the government and outside, the blow-up came not over an economic policy matter, but over the governor's pension. The government questioned the propriety of the procedure by which the

---

[8] In April 1958, Mr. Fleming welcomed the relaxation of monetary conditions in the previous months, and concluded that "few Canadians will weep at the bier of tight money." Hon. Donald Fleming, Speech to the Junior Chamber of Commerce, Hamilton, April 21, 1968 (mimeographed).

[9] "The Political Economics of the Bank of Canada," *Canadian Journal of Economics and Political Science*, November 1958, p. 472.

[10] Ibid., pp. 466-67.

[11] The case against the governor was detailed in H. Scott Gordon, *The Economists versus the Bank of Canada* (Toronto: Ryerson, 1961).

governor's pension had been increased, and at the end of May 1961, it demanded his resignation. His personal honor as well as his policies now at stake, the governor fought back, accusing the finance minister with having "deceived and misled Parliament and misrepresented my views." The political spectacle ended with Mr. Coyne's resignation on July 12, after special legislation had been introduced for his removal, and after he had presented his defense before a Senate committee.[12]

The return to a pegged rate. Having moved against the governor of the Bank of Canada, the government followed up with direct action to push down the high exchange value of the Canadian dollar which had accompanied the tight monetary conditions. In the June 1961 budget, the finance minister announced the intention to reduce interest rate differentials between Canada and the United States, and thereby reduce both the value of the Canadian dollar and the trade deficit. Further, the government declared that it would use the Exchange Fund Account to push the Canadian dollar to a significant discount by adding "substantial amounts to its holdings of United States dollars" if this proved necessary. In the event, substantial purchases were not needed: with the budget announcement, the Canadian dollar fell about 5 percent to a discount of over 3 percent in June while reserves rose by only $36 million (and the market effects of this intervention were partially offset by sales of $12 million in U.S. dollar forward contracts).[13] The decision of the Cana-

---

[12] For an account of the affair by a noted Canadian political reporter, see Peter Newman, *Renegade in Power: The Diefenbaker Years* (Toronto: McClelland and Stewart, 1963), Chapter 21.

[13] In my earlier study, *The Canadian Dollar, 1948-1962,* I raised questions about the legitimacy of Exchange Fund action to push down the rate in June, and took the $36 million accumulation to be the measure of that action (pp. 241, 259). This approach was found objectionable by A. F. Wynne Plumptre (a professor at the University of Toronto, previously with the Department of Finance) in *Exchange Rate Policy: Experience with Canada's Floating Rate* (Essays in International Finance #81, Princeton University, June 1970), p. 10:

> Several writers, examining the published statistics, have concluded that the Canadian authorities took aggressive action occasionally, and particularly in June 1961. However, I believe that, lacking at least some of the relevant information, in particular the position of the Exchange Fund on forward account, they may have been misled.

Mr. Plumptre is, of course, correct that the forward position should be considered; this is explained in greater detail in Chapter 4. The forward position has been published (in the Bank of Canada, *Statistical Summary Supplement,* 1961, p. 144) as a swing from +1.7 million at the end of May to —11.7 million at the end of June. Thus, forward operations soften my earlier point by reducing the intervention by one third; but the point remains.

dian government to use the fund to push the exchange rate to a target figure represented a major shift in government policy, and one which raised questions about the legitimate use of market intervention—a problem which will be considered in some detail in Chapter 6.

After the Canadian government intervened during the last half of 1961 to enforce a discount of 3¢ on the Canadian dollar, the situation changed dramatically in early 1962, and the objective came to be one of holding the Canadian dollar up, not down. In order to prevent a discount of more than 5¢, the authorities sold $461 million in U.S. funds between the beginning of 1962 and the end of April. By then, however, the system had become overloaded: while the government now wished the Canadian dollar to hold up in value, monetary ease continued, with Canadian-U.S. interest rate differentials remaining well below the rates of mid-1959 to mid-1961. (The seasonably adjusted money supply including savings deposits rose by an annual rate of more than 12 percent between March and April, and by 9 percent between April and May.) Speculative pressures began to build up at the end of April, and on May 2, the Canadian government pegged its currency at 92.5¢ U.S.

What had happened, apparently, is that the government had gotten the worst of both worlds. The Exchange Fund had been keeping the Canadian dollar from falling below 95¢ (U.S.) during the first four months of 1962, but market uncertainties were increased by the abrupt policy changes of the previous years and by the lack of a government commitment to the apparent 95¢ peg. For domestic reasons, monetary policy was being kept too expansive for this rate.

Nor did the decision at the beginning of May to retreat to an official peg of 92.5¢ eliminate the uncertainties. They were heightened by forthcoming elections of June 18, and the prospects of a minority government. Under the stress of the campaign, the government added to its own difficulties: the minister of agriculture announced that the cabinet had been split over the 92.5¢ rate, and he thought that it should be 90¢. And the election itself confirmed fears: the result was a minority government with Social Credit holding the balance of power. Speculative pressures grew, and in late June, the government felt forced to take emergency steps to protect the 92.5¢ peg. Monetary and fiscal policies were tightened; the government and central bank borrowed $650 million from the IMF and foreign central banks; and an extensive list of imports were subject to surcharges (removed in March 1963) ranging from 5 percent to

15 percent. The retreat from a flexible exchange rate had been anything but orderly.

The difficulties of the 1958-62 period left the impression that the flexible exchange rate had to be given up because it did not work. But this conclusion is unwarranted; the problem was not in the exchange rate mechanism, but rather in the inappropriate monetary policies which Canada followed. Indeed, the exchange rate mechanism may be considered to have worked *too* well: it added to the effectiveness of the inappropriate tight monetary policies, and contributed to the restrictive effects which these tight policies had on the Canadian economy.

4

THE PEGGED RATE, 1962-70: CANADA AND THE U.S. BALANCE OF PAYMENTS PROGRAMS

The circumstances surrounding the decisions of May-June 1962—when the capital outflow associated with easy money contributed to the crisis atmosphere—underlined the restraints within which monetary policy might have to operate with a fixed exchange rate. At that time, relatively easy monetary policies had to be abandoned in favor of high interest rates, in order that the drain on reserves might be halted. But, in the ensuing years, the Canadian international situation became much stronger. With the exceptions of the brief periods when U.S. balance of payments programs were applied to Canada, the predominant pressures on the Canadian dollar were up, not down. Thus, the major *potential* balance of payments restraint on Canadian policy lay in the possibility that Canadian authorities might be inhibited from following *tight* monetary policies. The possibilities of the potential restraint becoming an actual restriction on tighter monetary policies were increased by the commitments which Canada made not to increase its reserve levels in return for exemptions from U.S. restrictions on capital exports. Tighter monetary policies would have complicated the fulfillment of these commitments.

This is not to suggest that Canadian domestic policy would actually have been greatly different during 1962-70 if there had been a flexible exchange rate. Indeed, the policies in Canada were reasonably similar overall to those in the United States because of domestic conditions in Canada, and not because of any particular external restraint. The major consequence of the reserve commitment was a series of temporizing ad hoc arrangements, which kept the Canadian exchange rate pegged, and thus prevented an appreciation which would have partially offset the domestic inflationary effects of domestic policies.

U.S. Balance of Payments Programs and Canada

The story of the United States balance of payments programs, as seen from Canada, has been one of abrupt changes in the conditions under which Canada has had access to the United States capital market, followed by balance of payments problems in Canada, followed by an appeal for exemption from the U.S. programs, followed by the granting of exemption subject to certain conditions. There are three main chapters in this story: the U.S. interest equalization tax announced in July of 1963, the "voluntary" balance of payments program beginning in February 1965, and the mandatory balance of payments program announced at the beginning of 1968.

The interest equalization tax, 1963. The objective of the interest equalization tax was to reduce the capital outflow from the United States by increasing the costs of raising capital (by about one percentage point). This was done with a graduated tax, running from 2.75 percent on debt obligations with three years until maturity to 15 percent on long-term debts and equities.

Canada had historically been the major foreign borrower in the New York market, and had continued to be so into the early sixties. Of the $2.15 billion total in new issues of foreign securities in the 1960-62 period, over $1 billion had gone to Canada. In the first two quarters of 1963, immediately prior to the interest equalization tax, the contrast between Canadian and Western European new issues was dramatic: $632 million for Canada and only $119 million for Western Europe. Nevertheless, little attention seems to have been paid to the potential effects of the tax on Canada. Indeed, the tax came as a "surprise" to Canadian officials.[1]

Immediately with the announcement of the tax on July 18, 1963, "a wave of uncertainty and apprehension swept through the Canadian financial markets."[2] On July 18 and 19, the Exchange Fund Account suffered substantial losses, and bond prices sagged. Urgent consultations ensued, with the U.S. administration undertaking to ask for authority in the proposed tax legislation to grant an exemption for Canadian new issues (but not outstanding securities). In return, Canada declared that it would be neither her "desire nor intention to increase her foreign exchange reserves through the proceeds of borrowings in the United States."[3]

---

[1] Bank of Canada, *Annual Report*, 1963, p. 4.

[2] Ibid.

[3] Ibid., p. 6.

The voluntary guidelines, 1965. In February of 1965, about 500 large U.S. nonfinancial corporations were asked to make a maximum effort to increase the net balance of (a) their exports of goods and services, and (b) their repatriations of earnings from the developed countries, less (c) their capital outflows to the developed countries.[4] While the U.S. program asked companies to repatriate earnings and short-term financial assets in Canada, the U.S. government declared that it did "not anticipate cutbacks in Canadian direct investments." [5]

Following the U.S. steps of February 1965, the minister of finance asked the Canadian chartered banks to prevent their net asset positions vis-à-vis U.S. residents from falling below the level at the end of 1964. As U.S. residents withdrew U.S. deposits from Canadian banks in response to the American guidelines, the banks met only part of the drain by liquidating investments in the United States. During 1965, they drew $955 million from other countries by liquidating assets and increasing liabilities. In this way Canadian action reinforced the U.S. objective of drawing excess dollars from Europe.

With the growing concern over the balance of payments in the United States, a decision was made at the end of 1965 to extend the request for voluntary foreign direct investment restraint to cover Canada. In addition to a general appeal to corporations to continue to maximize their balance of payments contributions through export expansion, a specific guideline was introduced for direct investment abroad. Each of about 900 corporations was requested to keep its average investment abroad during 1965 and 1966 to no more than 135 percent of the 1962-64 average—including retained earnings as well as new capital flows.

A major objective of the U.S. direct investment program was to push the financing of investments into foreign capital markets. This caused considerable concern in Canada lest the subsidiaries of U.S. corporations push Canadian businesses out of their positions in the Canadian capital market. In commenting on the long-term financing of American subsidiaries, the minister of finance on February 2, 1966 expressed the hope and expectation that "there will be no abnormal recourse to the Canadian capital market, but if there were the Government would have to decide what action to take." [6] The

---

[4] Council of Economic Advisers, *Annual Report*, 1966, p. 166.

[5] Commerce Secretary Connor, Statement of March 12, 1965. This statement, and a number of other documents on the early balance of payments guidelines, may be found in George P. Shultz and Robert Z. Aliber, eds., *Guidelines, Informal Controls, and the Market Place* (University of Chicago Press, 1966), App. B.

[6] As quoted in Bank of Canada, *Annual Report*, 1965, p. 10.

governor of the Bank of Canada informed the heads of the chartered banks that if they found themselves unable to meet in full the demands for business loans from their credit-worthy customers as a result of the demands arising out of the U.S. guidelines, he expected them to "continue to look after the customers who had relied on them in the past for their credit needs."[7]

While there was a potential for a rather sharp conflict between Canadian and U.S. interests—indeed, U.S. pressures on their corporations to increase exports and repatriate dividends from their foreign subsidiaries led the Canadian government to counter with "guiding principles of good corporate behaviour" at the end of March 1966[8]—the policy enunciated by the minister of finance on March 16, 1966 worked in the direction both of ensuring the place of Canadian domestic corporations in the Canadian capital market, and of preventing a leakage of American funds through Canada. Such a leakage might have occurred if Canadian funds had been used to purchase the securities of European subsidiaries of U.S. corporations, with the vacuum in the Canadian capital market being filled by funds borrowed in New York under the interest equalization tax exemption. (U.S. citizens could not purchase the securities of European subsidiaries of U.S. companies without paying the tax.) Any such leakage would clearly have defeated the U.S. objective of pushing the financing of their subsidiaries into foreign markets. The March statement of the finance minister requested

> all Canadian investors, including financial institutions such as banks, life insurance companies, and trust and loan companies, as well as other corporations, pension funds and individuals, not to acquire securities . . . which are issued by United States corporations or their non-Canadian subsidiaries and which are subject to the United States interest equalization tax if purchased by United States residents.[9]

In addition to the tightening of the foreign direct investment guidelines, the United States in late 1965 introduced a precise guide-

---

[7] Ibid.

[8] Which called, among other things, for the searching out and development of Canadian procurement sources, and the retention of earnings sufficient to support the growth of Canadian subsidiaries. The Watkins Report suggested that the Canadian principles should be further developed and made mandatory. See *Foreign Ownership and the Structure of Canadian Industry,* Report of the Task Force on the Structure of Canadian Industry, Ottawa, January 1968, pp. 233, 337.

[9] The March 16, 1966 Statement of Finance Minister Sharp, and a number of other documents related to the U.S. balance of payments programs as they affected Canada, may be found in Bank of Canada, *Annual Report,* 1968, pp. 64-73.

line for the purchase of long-term foreign securities by American nonbank[10] financial institutions (insurance companies, etc.), limiting the increase to 5 percent of the September 1965 figure. Because of Canadian concern over the effects of this guideline, Canada was exempted, again in return for a commitment on the Canadian side. The "target" figure for Canadian reserves was to be reduced to $2,600 million from the $2,700 million agreed to at the time of the original interest equalization tax exemption.[11] (Canada's net creditor position with the IMF, which had been zero until late 1964, was included in the $2,600 million "target," which was further reduced to $2,550 million in May of 1966 in conjunction with the increase of $47.5 million in the Canadian gold subscription in the IMF.)

In order to reach the new lower target by the end of 1966, the Canadian government agreed that, if necessary, it would repatriate securities held in the United States. This was in fact done in 1966, when Canada purchased over $150 million of its own securities in the United States, and about $25 million of U.S.-pay bonds of the International Bank for Reconstruction and Development.

The mandatory program, 1968. The voluntary guidelines were retained through 1966 and 1967, with the direct investment ceiling being lowered at the end of 1966 from 135 percent to 120 percent of the 1962-64 average. The U.S. balance of payments became an increasing source of concern, particularly with the monetary disturbances associated with the British devaluation in late 1967. By the standards of the time, the U.S. deficit was high in the fourth quarter of 1967—$1.8 billion on the liquidity basis and $1.0 billion on official settlements (seasonally adjusted). The U.S. government responded on January 1, 1968, by announcing a major balance of payments program, with the most important feature being the transformation of the foreign direct investment restrictions to a mandatory basis.

For the developed countries including Canada to which U.S. capital flows were considered essential, capital outflows plus reinvested earnings were to be limited to 65 percent of the annual average of 1965-66. The Canadian dollar quickly came under pressure: about $350 million was lost in reserves of U.S. dollars during January (with $250 million being replenished by a swap with the Federal Reserve). The Canadian $426 million in the IMF was withdrawn in February,

---

[10] Guidelines were also applied to U.S. banks.

[11] Bank of Canada, *Annual Report*, 1965, p. 9.

and the Exchange Fund Account sold $455 million in forward U.S. dollars in the first three months of 1968.

On January 21, 1968, the U.S. Treasury issued a statement stressing that the balance of payments program was not intended to produce abnormal transfers of funds from Canada. Then, in the face of a continuing pressure on the Canadian dollar, Canada was exempted from substantially all U.S. balance of payments measures on March 7. In return, Canada agreed to prevent itself from being used as a "pass-through for funds headed from the U.S. to other foreign countries," and undertook to invest her entire holdings of U.S. dollars (apart from working balances) in U.S. government non-liquid securities.

The changing Canadian balance of payments position. In quick order, Canada swung from a need to protect its reserve position to a need to avoid an overrun of the reserve target established in return for exemptions from the U.S. programs. There were several reasons for this. The balance of payments programs exemptions, of course, were one; Canada continued to raise sizable amounts of capital in New York, with new issues of bonds in the United States amounting to $1,355 million during 1968, or slightly more than in 1967. But, more important, there were unusual sources of strength in the Canadian balance of payments. Canada had typically run large current account deficits, ranging from $424 million (1964) to $1,233 million (1960) during the nineteen sixties. Indeed, the need to cover continuing current deficits had provided urgency to the Canadian desires to gain exemption from the U.S. payments programs. With the tourist attraction provided by Expo '67, it had been expected that the current deficit would drop in 1967, and this had in fact happened; the deficit declined by $663 million to a 1967 figure of $499 million, with an increase of almost $500 million being registered in tourist earnings. But, what was not anticipated, the current account improvement continued into 1968, even though tourist earnings fell back. With a booming United States demand drawing in imports from all over the world, the Canadian current deficit with the U.S. declined from $1,342 million in 1967 to $792 million in 1968, and there was a corresponding decline in the overall Canadian current deficit, from $499 million to $60 million.

An equally important movement, contributing another half billion dollars to the Canadian balance of payments, resulted from Canadian borrowings outside the United States. In 1967, these borrowings had amounted to only $55 million; in 1968, they soared to

$540 million as a result of very tight monetary conditions in North America and relatively greater supplies of funds in Europe.

The relaxation of the Canadian reserve commitment. These European borrowings introduced a significant complication into the commitments which the Canadian government had undertaken as a condition for exemption from the restrictions of the U.S. balance of payments program. In particular, the reserve target had been introduced as an assurance that Canada would not go to the United States market for more capital than was needed to cover current account deficits. Now, however, with Europe being a significant source of funds for Canada, steps by Canada to discourage the inflow of capital could operate against the U.S. payments objective of reducing European holdings of U.S. dollars. Also, incidentally, they could cause a statistical deterioration in the U.S. liquidity balance, since Canada had undertaken to put her reserves in excess of working balances into nonliquid U.S. government securities. In a sense, then, it was not in the United States interest to hold the Canadian government to its reserve limit.

Matters came to a head toward the end of the year, as reserve increases and the existence of the upper reserve "target" threatened to put severe limitations on Canadian monetary policy. Letters were again exchanged between Washington and Ottawa, in which the U.S. secretary of the treasury noted that, while Canada had declared her intention not to increase her reserves through borrowings in the United States,

> implementation of this principle does not require that Canada's reserve level be limited to any particular figure. We are well aware of Canada's need for flexibility with respect to reserve levels in order to accommodate the adoption of monetary policy to the changing needs of its domestic economy. . . . In recent times capital markets in other countries have developed a capacity which has attracted borrowers from many countries. Canadian authorities have taken advantage of these expanding capital markets to raise funds in substantial quantities. These developments now offer Canada an alternative means of achieving an increase in its reserves whenever Canadian authorities believe this to be desirable.[12]

[12] Secretary Fowler's letter, and Finance Minister Benson's reply, may be found in Bank of Canada, *Annual Report*, 1968, pp. 67-69.

In effect, then, the reserve "target" would no longer constitute a limit within which Canadian reserves were expected to remain.

An evaluation of the overall techniques and objectives of the U.S. balance of payments program clearly lies far beyond the scope of this paper, but it may be interesting to speculate whether the relaxation of the Canadian reserve ceiling reflected a shift in the general strategy of U.S. payments programs. Behind the reserve ceiling were the assumptions that the U.S. balance of payments position had to be improved, that Canada should be looked on as part of the outside world, and that any flow of funds to Canada should be kept to the minimum necessary. While the need to improve the American payments position continued to be stressed, the pass-through commitments and associated balance of payments exemptions seemed to be based on the view that North America constituted a single capital market, and that the important objective was not so much to keep dollars within the United States as it was to keep them out of Europe.

Certainly, with the establishment of the two-tier gold system in mid-March of 1968, there was less immediate pressure on the United States to look on the balance of payments problem as one of preventing the imminent collapse of the gold exchange standard. It would have been a natural consequence for there to be an increase in the importance of problems of monetary management associated with large accumulations of dollars in European hands. As seen from the United States, Canadian steps to decrease capital inflows (e.g., through lower interest rates) and thus stay within the reserve ceiling would tend to have opposite effects on the North American balance vis-à-vis Europe, on the one hand, and the United States balance of payments, on the other. The North American balance would be made worse; the basic American balance, better (because of the lesser flow of U.S. funds to Canada, subject to qualifications noted below). The relaxation of the Canadian reserve ceiling may therefore be interpreted as a step towards a unified North American capital market.

Unfortunately, however, the complexities of the U.S. balance of payments program rule out any categorical conclusion regarding a "common capital market." It would be quite possible to explain the willingness to see the Canadian reserve ceiling breached, not on the ground that U.S. policy makers were looking at the North American capital market as a whole, but on the ground that a breaching of the ceiling was desirable from the narrower viewpoint of the U.S. balance of payments. The Canadian commitment to place reserves in nonliquid U.S. governments, and the quaint treatment of these nonliquid governments in the U.S. balance of payments statistics, meant that lower Canadian interest rates aimed at suppressing reserve increases would have made the accounted U.S. liquidity balance of payments *worse* (by reducing European capital flows to Canada, and therefore reducing official Canadian flows to the United States).

Canadian Domestic Policies and the Balance of Payments Restraint

One of the major rationales for capital controls such as those in the U.S. balance of payments programs is that, in a world of fixed exchange rates and otherwise highly mobile capital, such controls will provide a degree of monetary independence. Canada, however, gained exemptions from the U.S. programs on the grounds of its historic need for U.S. capital. The conditions accepted, in particular the reserve ceiling, had the potential effect of severely limiting Canadian monetary independence, over and above the normal restraints resulting from fixed exchange rates. How severe in fact was this limit?

The most obvious point that arises from a quick overview of Canadian policy is that, with the possible exception of the period immediately prior to the floating of the rate in 1970, the most notable external complications for Canadian policy occurred as a result of the *initiation* of U.S. balance of payments programs in 1963 and 1968, and not as a result of the reserve ceiling.

Disturbances associated with the initiation of U.S. programs. In the summer of 1963, with the introduction of the U.S. interest equalization tax, there was a quick downward movement in Canadian bond prices, although not nearly so sharp as had accompanied the troubles in mid-1962. Even after the more acute pressures were relieved by the July 21, 1963 announcement that the administration would ask for the power to exempt new issues from the new tax, considerable uncertainty existed in the markets as to the actual outcome in Congress, and it was not until the proclamation of the exemption in September 1964 and the consequent spurt of new Canadian issues that the interest rate differential narrowed back towards its June 1963 level.

The Canadian authorities considered the interest rate changes following the interest equalization tax announcement to be undesirable; indeed, the disorganized state of the bond market precipitated the request for a Canadian exemption. In order to reduce the downward pressures on Canadian bond prices,[13] the Bank of Canada bought

[13] Bank of Canada, *Annual Report*, 1963, p. 6.

Figure 3

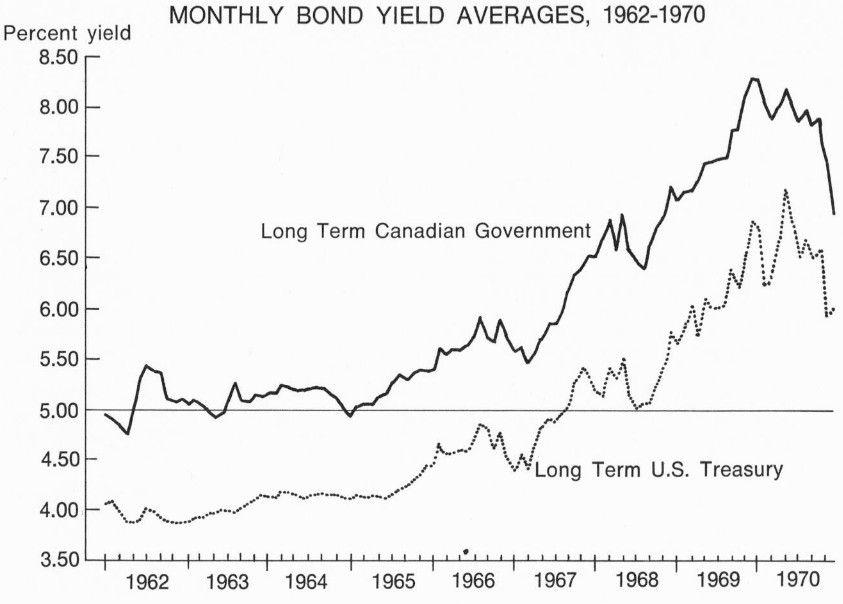

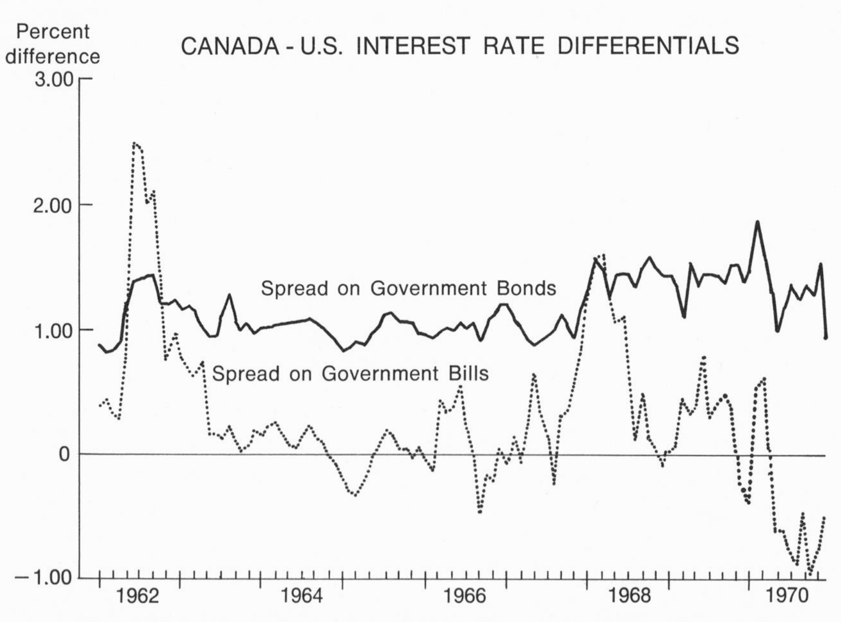

Source: *Federal Reserve Bulletin; Bank of Canada Statistical Summary.*

bonds, thereby keeping up the reserve base. The tax resulted in somewhat higher interest rates than were deemed desirable for domestic considerations, but there was little, if any, effect on the overall monetary aggregates except in the month immediately after the tax was announced.

In early 1968, with the introduction of the mandatory direct investment program which until March was applied to Canada, there was a sharp reduction in Canadian reserves. At the end of October 1967, Canadian reserves (including the net creditor position in the IMF) had been $2,569.1 million, or very slightly above the agreed target. Reserves had declined somewhat—by about $50 million—by the end of the year, with the monetary disturbances resulting from the British devaluation presumably being a factor. With the introduction of the U.S. mandatory program, the Canadian international position deteriorated sharply, with holdings of gold and dollars falling slightly ($23 million) in the first three months of 1968 in spite of the borrowings of $250 million (U.S.) by the Bank of Canada under its swap with the Federal Reserve Bank of New York, the drawing of $426 million from the IMF, the repayment to Canada of $35 million under the GAB, and the sale of $455 million by the Exchange Fund Account on the forward market. The major deterioration of the Canadian balance of payments involved a decline of almost $400 million in long-term capital inflows and an increase of over $300 million in short-term capital outflows between the last quarter of 1967 and the first quarter of 1968.

During the first half of 1968, the Bank of Canada gave priority to the defense of the Canadian dollar.[14] The bank rate, which had been raised a percentage point to 6 percent after the British devaluation in November, was raised again by 1 percent on January 22, and by another half point on March 15. Canadian interest rates rose, not only absolutely, but also in comparison with American rates. The rate of growth of the money supply in the first quarter of 1968 was significantly lower than the rate in the surrounding periods. In March, the money supply[15] was only 3.1 percent (at an annual rate of increase) above January, and 3.7 percent above December 1967. In contrast, the money supply grew at a rate of 16.1 percent from December 1966 to December 1967.

---

[14] Bank of Canada, *Annual Report*, 1968, p. 8.

[15] Currency outside banks and Canadian chartered bank deposits held by the general public; average of Wednesdays.

Figure 4

CANADIAN DOLLAR IN TERMS OF THE UNITED STATES DOLLAR

1962-1970

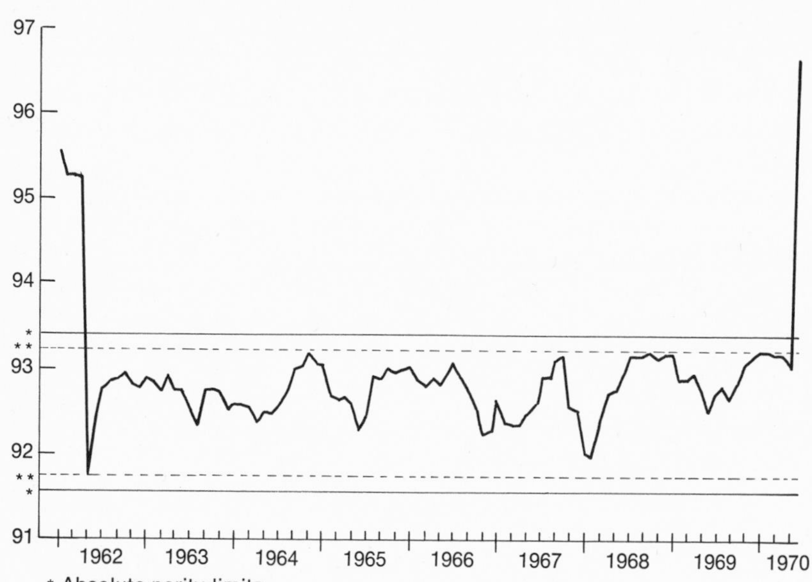

* Absolute parity limits.

** Limits at which Exchange Fund Account undertook to sell or buy U.S. funds without limit.

NINETY DAY FORWARD DIFFERENTIAL

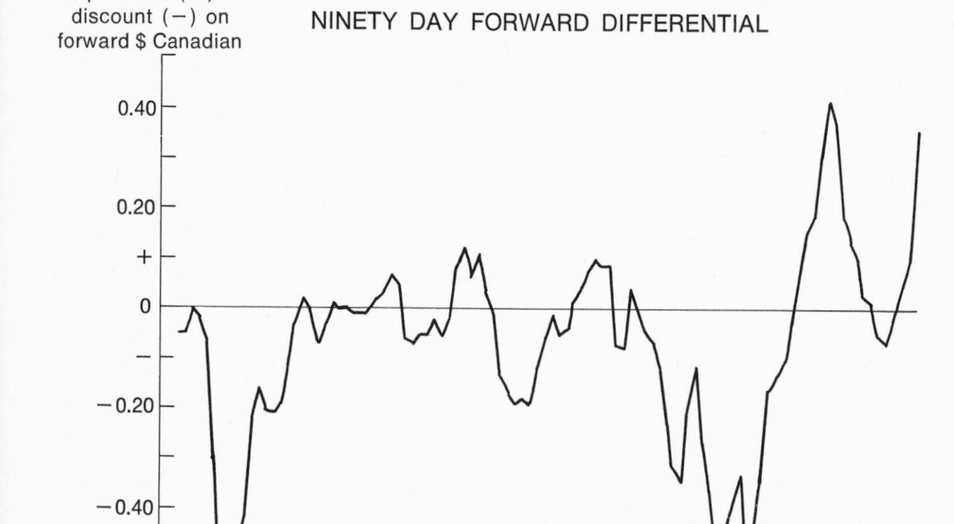

Source: *Bank of Canada Statistical Summary.*

Here we have a classic illustration of an external restraint on monetary policy: a foreign disturbance leading to a negative response of capital flows, a loss of reserves, a tightening of the money supply, and a rise in interest rates. During the early part of 1968, Canada was clearly subject to an external restraint,[16] and when the exchange crisis came to an end, the more expansive policies considered appropriate for domestic conditions were reestablished.[17] In the light of price increases, it has been debated whether the very high rates of monetary growth for 1968 as a whole were undesirable (and whether, by implication, the external restraint was in retrospect good). The answer is unclear, inasmuch as Canada in 1967 entered a period of combined inflation and high unemployment rates, a dilemma not encountered in an acute form in the United States until 1970.

The reserve target. For the rest of the 1963-68 period, of course, the external restraint was not toward tighter policies, but *potentially* towards more expansive ones, as Canada was committed to an upper reserve target, with reserves usually being close to and at times modestly exceeding the target. An evaluation of the practical restraint of this target on Canadian policy requires some knowledge of the policies which would otherwise have been followed by authorities in the absence of the restraint, and these cannot be discovered with any degree of precision. But, before considering this question of adjustments in Canadian domestic monetary policies, attention should be turned to the various expedients which may be used to escape the effects of the "reserve target" which seems, at first glance, to impose a very rigid restraint on Canadian policies.

1. *Expedients to prevent the piercing of the target.* In order to avoid major shifts in monetary policies which an adherence to the reserve target might otherwise necessitate, the Canadian authorities had a number of temporizing expedients open to them, involving direct steps to reduce the net capital inflow. It was seen above that, at the time of the 1965 Canadian exemption from the U.S. balance of payments program, the Canadian government declared its willingness to repatriate its own securities held in the United States, and repur-

---

[16] In referring to the 1 percent increase in the bank rate on January 21, Finance Minister Sharp said, "I believe this move was appropriate and prudent to protect the Canadian dollar. . . . I regret, as we all will regret, that external circumstances have made this step necessary." Hon. Mitchell Sharp, Statement to the House of Commons on the Position of the Canadian Dollar, January 22, 1968 (mimeographed).

[17] Bank of Canada, *Annual Report*, 1968, p. 8.

chases were in fact made during 1966 and 1967. In addition to these repurchases, Canadian officials from time to time made efforts to keep the net inflow of capital down by suggestions to borrowers that they reduce their issues on the United States market. Thus, for example, the Canadian authorities in early December 1964 suggested to provincial governments that it would be helpful if they made little use of the U.S. market for the time being.

The forward market might have been used as a third possible method of temporarily keeping down Canadian reserves. By buying U.S. dollars forward, the Canadian authorities could have depressed the forward rate on the Canadian dollar, thereby providing arbitrageurs with an incentive to buy forward Canadian dollars and sell spot Canadian dollars, and thus reduce official holdings of U.S. dollars. The record does not, however, suggest that this method was used extensively, at least not until late 1968. Prior to that time, on only three occasions [18] following the initial Canadian reserve commitment in mid-1963 did the forward U.S. dollar holdings of the Exchange Fund Account exceed $80 million. And on these three occasions—September 1963, March 1964, and August 1965—there was not much difficulty in remaining below the reserve target. On the contrary, the forward market got its greatest workout when the Canadian dollar was under downward pressure in early 1968 following the introduction of the U.S. mandatory controls. The Exchange Fund Account sold U.S. dollars forward at that time (totaling $454.4 million by the end of March), providing an incentive for funds to move to Canada.

The forward market was, however, apparently used to keep Canadian reserves below the target figure in October 1968, when the Exchange Fund Account held $134.5 million in forward U.S. dollars. Most of this position ($117 million) was maintained through November, but this was not sufficiently great to prevent the ceiling from being pierced in that month.

2. *The reserve target as a restraint to Canadian monetary policy.* So much for the steps taken to suppress reserves directly in order to remain within the target figure. How much did the reserve commitment deflect Canadian monetary policy from the path it would otherwise have followed?

Statements by the Bank of Canada suggest that, at least until late 1968 when the reserve target caused such problems that it was

[18] That is, at only three ends of the month; only end of the month data are available. Bank of Canada, *Statistical Summary, Supplement.*

greatly modified, the size of Canadian reserves was not a major complication in monetary policy. Following the interest equalization tax announcement and the Canadian reserve commitment in 1963, reserves remained comfortably below the ceiling until the Canadian exemption for new issues was actually proclaimed in the fall of 1964. And in the fall of 1964, the major international complication on the Canadian monetary scene came not from the United States, but from the heavy selling of Canadian securities in Canada following the November 24th increase of the Bank of England's lending rate from 5 percent to 7 percent. During 1965, the Bank of Canada observed, Canada "had to take the agreement regarding reserves into account," but was "able to pursue a monetary policy which in its broad lines was appropriate to the requirements of our domestic situation as it developed." [19] In 1966, with interest rates moving up very rapidly in the credit crunch in the United States, "the Bank of Canada became concerned about the degree of restraint that was developing in financial markets." In the face of conflicting considerations—with evidence accumulating that the growth of aggregate demand was moderating, while, on the other hand, cost pressures were continuing to increase—the bank "considered that the appropriate policy was for it to offer considerable resistance to a further tightening of credit conditions without, however, attempting to prevent all further upward movement in interest rates." Thus, for *domestic* reasons, it was considered desirable to keep interest rates from rising more than they were simultaneously rising in the United States, and the reserve ceiling does not seem to have played a significant role in pushing the bank towards more monetary expansion. Indeed, if anything, international considerations seem to have worked slightly in the opposite direction: the bank mentions that it "of course had to be concerned with the maintenance of credit conditions favourable to an adequate capital inflow." [20]

During 1967, the Bank of Canada allowed a rapid rate of monetary expansion—over 16 percent for the year.[21] The tighter financial conditions that a less rapid rate would have implied were considered undesirable, "having regard to both domestic considerations and the need at the time to avoid excessive capital inflows." [22] This may be

---

[19] Bank of Canada, *Annual Report*, 1965, p. 8.

[20] All the quotations for 1966 are from Bank of Canada, *Annual Report*, 1966, p. 5.

[21] December 1966 to December 1967 changes in currency and deposits held by general public.

[22] Bank of Canada, *Annual Report*, 1967, p. 10.

interpreted as meaning that, although a rapid rate of monetary expansion was considered desirable domestically, the reserve ceiling may have increased the degree to which monetary authorities were willing to allow the money supply to expand.

All in all, the statements of the Bank of Canada suggest that the reserve ceiling did not significantly alter the course of Canadian monetary policy. It was, nevertheless, an annoyance, and one that could not be entirely avoided with the use of debt prepayment and other direct Canadian actions affecting net capital flows.[23] The discomfort was reflected in Mr. Rasminsky's observation that "A situation in which Canada needs to import a great deal of capital is inherently unsatisfactory, and there is no easy or satisfactory way of dealing with it."[24]

Changes in the mix of monetary and fiscal policies. A simple review of the statements of the Bank of Canada does not necessarily give a complete picture of the influence of international restraints on Canadian monetary policy. It is, however, useful in evaluating the effects of the external restraint during this very difficult period of economic policy, since it is hard to tell otherwise what policies the Bank might have followed in the absence of an external restraint. During the last half of the sixties, policy makers were trapped between two powerful and conflicting forces—the need to stop inflation, on the one hand, and the desire to prevent high unemployment, on the other. The dilemma appeared three years earlier in Canada than in the United States: beginning in 1967, and lasting through 1969, Canada suffered from a three-year period of generally rising inflation rates, and generally rising unemployment. (See Figure 11, page 68, below.) The same dilemma did not show up in such an obvious form until 1970 in the United States.

It is of course impossible to come to any categorical conclusions on the basis of a simple comparison of the policies in the two countries. But such a comparison may be useful. If we look at two of the standard policy measures—the high employment budget position for fiscal policy, and the rate of change of the money supply for monetary policy—the reliance on monetary and fiscal policies in the two countries has been considerably different over the past decade. Up to the

---

[23] Substantially similar conclusions are reached by Robert M. Dunn, *Canada's Experience with Fixed and Flexible Exchange Rates in a North American Capital Market* (Washington: Canadian-American Committee, National Planning Association, May 1971), pp. 33-40.

[24] Bank of Canada, *Annual Report*, 1965, p. 10.

Figure 5

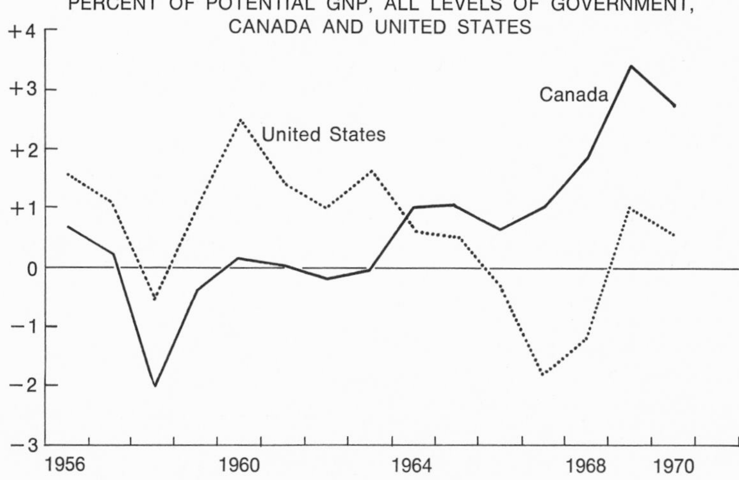

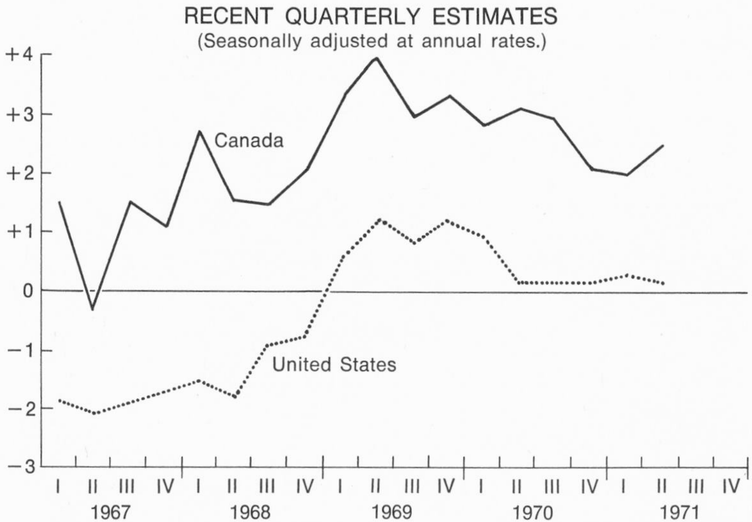

Note: High employment is defined for this purpose as the level of employment associated with 3.8 percent unemployment. The high-employment budget position is calculated on a national accounts basis and is derived by estimating the change in revenues that would be realized at high employment; expenditures are assumed to remain unchanged.

Source: Economic Council of Canada, based on data from Dominion Bureau of Statistics, U.S. Department of Commerce, and U.S. Council of Economic Advisers.

time of the U.S. tax cut in 1964, the Canadian full employment budget was more stimulative than the American, generally being in deficit or close to balance, in contrast to the U.S. full employment surpluses.[25] After 1964, however, the picture changed dramatically, with Canada moving to significant full employment surplus while the U.S. slid into a large deficit which lasted until 1969 (Figure 5). Between 1962 and 1964, Canadian rates of monetary expansion were somewhat less than those in the United States, and thereafter somewhat greater (Figure 6). About 1964, therefore, there was a change in the relative policy postures of the two countries, with the United States moving to the more expansive fiscal policy, and Canada to the more expansive monetary stance.

Two interconnected lines of argument related to the Canadian balance of payments might be used to explain in part this relative

Figure 6

CHANGES IN SUPPLY OF MONEY, CANADA AND UNITED STATES
(year-over-year)

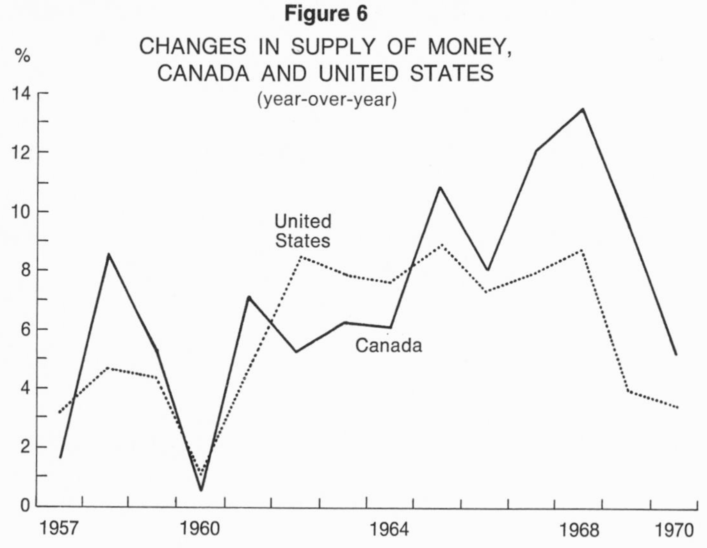

Note: The supply of money is here defined as follows:
Canada—currency outside banks and Canadian dollar chartered bank deposits held by the general public.
United States—currency plus demand deposits, plus time deposits of commercial and mutual savings banks.

Source: Economic Council of Canada, from data of the Bank of Canada and the Federal Reserve Board.

[25] The Canadian full employment budget estimates are those of the Economic Council of Canada, based on 3.8 percent unemployment. There is some question about the use of this figure, as 3.8 percent unemployment may not have been sustainable because of the very large increases in the Canadian labor force in the later 1960s. In his *Submission to the Senate Standing Committee on National Finance*, June 29, 1971, p. 7, Finance Minister Benson expressed reservations about the high employment budget concept.

change in policy emphasis. A change towards a relatively less expansionary fiscal policy and a relatively more expansionary monetary policy tends to reduce demand pressures on the financial markets. Thus, the shift in the relative Canadian position during 1964-67 reduced the attraction of funds to Canada. In addition to the methods for keeping within the reserve ceiling which were discussed above, the reserve agreement may have encouraged a shift in the relative mix of Canadian policy. Alternatively, it might be observed that, quite independent of any reserve ceiling, the Canadian authorities have had a long-standing desire to reduce Canada's dependence on U.S. capital, and this desire would adequately explain Canadian decisions to moderate the inflow of capital through adjustments in the policy mix. We are therefore left with an uncertain conclusion. Canadian changes in policy mix were consistent with the desire to stay within the reserve ceiling, but they could be explained on other grounds as well.

The Puzzle of 1969

During the 1963-68 period, the most conspicuous external influences on monetary policy came as a result of the periodic changes in U.S. balance of payments programs: the effects of the U.S. mandatory program, combined with those of the British devaluation, were particularly marked in the brief but sharp reduction in the rate of Canadian monetary expansion in the first quarter of 1968. During much of the rest of the period, the restraint was at least potentially on the other side, with the reserve ceiling and the continuing capital mobility resulting from Canadian exemptions placing a limit on how tight Canadian monetary policy could be compared to U.S. policy. The evidence suggests, however, that this restraint was not severe in practice, and was largely avoided by special Canadian steps such as the repatriation of Canadian bonds.

Perhaps the most interesting question regarding Canadian monetary dependence during the 1962-70 period of fixed exchange rates concerns the history of 1969, after the relaxation of the Canadian commitment to a reserve ceiling, and during a period when there were no sharp, disturbing changes in the U.S. payments programs. During 1969, there was an abrupt shift in Canadian monetary conditions toward restraint—more abrupt, indeed, than had occurred as a result of the balance of payments disturbance of early 1968.

In 1969, the pattern of monetary expansion in Canada was quite similar to that in the United States—one might say remarkably

Figure 7

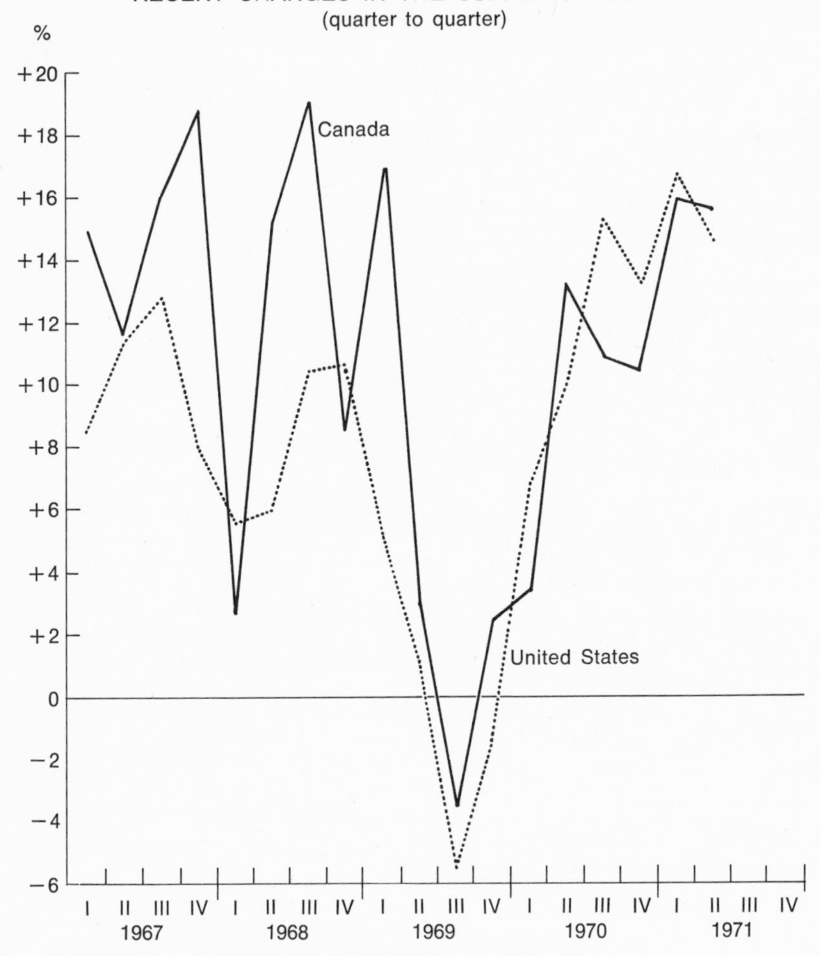

* Seasonally adjusted at annual rates.

Note: The supply of money is here defined as follows:

Canada—currency outside banks and Canadian dollar chartered bank deposits held by the general public.

United States—currency plus demand deposits, plus time deposits of commercial and mutual savings banks.

Source: Economic Council of Canada, from data of the Bank of Canada and the Federal Reserve Board.

similar, had it not been for the different pattern of the first quarter (Figure 7). It is hard to attribute this similar behavior to an external restraint in the classical sense: the Canadian balance of payments was certainly strong enough to have permitted the Canadians to move less abruptly to tighter money in 1969 than did the United States. It is true that Canada did follow policies somewhat less restrictive than would have been necessary to keep the international position completely firm; there was a small decrease in Canadian reserves between January and July, and the Canadian dollar softened from 93.22¢ in January to a figure just slightly in excess of the official par in July (92.54¢, average of noon rates). Furthermore, the Bank of Canada requested the chartered banks to accept a temporary ceiling on swapped deposits in the middle of July in order to limit the impact of high Eurodollar rates on the Canadian market. But there was considerably more leeway for a lowering of the high reserve level, or for a decline in the value of the Canadian dollar into the lower half of its pegged band. The external restraint did not bar less restrictive policies in Canada. Rather, the tightness of Canadian monetary conditions which accompanied the U.S. shift reflected a similar response to the domestic problem of inflation. In explaining monetary policy during 1969, the Bank of Canada stressed the importance of attacking the inflationary expectations which had come to predominate.[26]

However, to suggest that the similarity between Canadian and U.S. monetary policies during 1969 can be explained on the basis of similar responses to similar domestic conditions would be going too far: conditions in the two countries differed noticeably at the beginning of 1969. In the United States, the strong expansive forces had continued without abatement through 1968, with the unemployment rate drifting down and inflationary pressures gathering steam. An abrupt change could be recommended in the United States as a necessary step to modify the strong forces of demand which had been gathering for years; not so in Canada. While prices continued to rise at a disagreeable rate, unemployment had increased since the second half of 1966, and it was not particularly easy to see the ground for a sharp restrictive move on the demand side. The common North American policy can be more clearly explained for the U.S. than for Canada. While categorical evaluations of policy become difficult during periods of high unemployment and high inflation, it does seem that Canadian monetary policy may have been carried along with developing U.S. monetary conditions and with developing alarm in

[26] Bank of Canada, *Annual Report*, 1969, pp. 5-13.

the United States over the continuing buoyancy of demand in spite of the tax surcharge of 1968. What may have been at work here is a policy restraint more broad and pervasive than that which comes directly from capital flows and the pressures which they put on the authorities to protect the reserve position—a restraint resulting from the powerful influence of a larger neighbor nation.

5
THE RECENT FLOAT, 1970–

Apart from temporary aberrations, the Canadian reserve position had remained relatively stable during the 1963-69 period. Early in 1970, however, Canadian reserves began to rise rapidly, increasing during the first five months by more than $850 million (not including Special Drawing Rights allocations), plus an additional $360 million in forward contracts.

The immediate problem precipitated by the balance of payments strength was that of financing the $850 million of reserve accumulations: the Exchange Fund Account's holdings of Canadian dollars became severely depleted by late May. In a sense this was a technical problem: reserve accumulation could have been financed by borrowing from the Bank of Canada. Such a policy, indeed, would have approximated the classical adjustment mechanism foreseen with fixed exchange rates, with surpluses resulting in monetary expansion, hence the expansion of demand, and hence compensating increases in imports. But the prospect of a major monetary expansion over and above that already taking place (Figure 7) was distasteful to the Canadian authorities in the light of the continuing problem of inflation. In order to avoid being driven into an inappropriately expansive monetary policy, the government allowed the Canadian dollar to float upward at the beginning of June.

The earlier abandonment of fixed exchange rates, in 1950, was essentially the result of large scale inflows of capital from the United States. In 1970, in contrast, the upward pressures were broadly based. Historically, the Canadian current account balance had been negative, with deficits running to more than $1 billion in the mid-1960s, and to $750 million in 1969. Beginning with the first quarter of 1970, there was a big swing of the current account into surplus

Figure 8

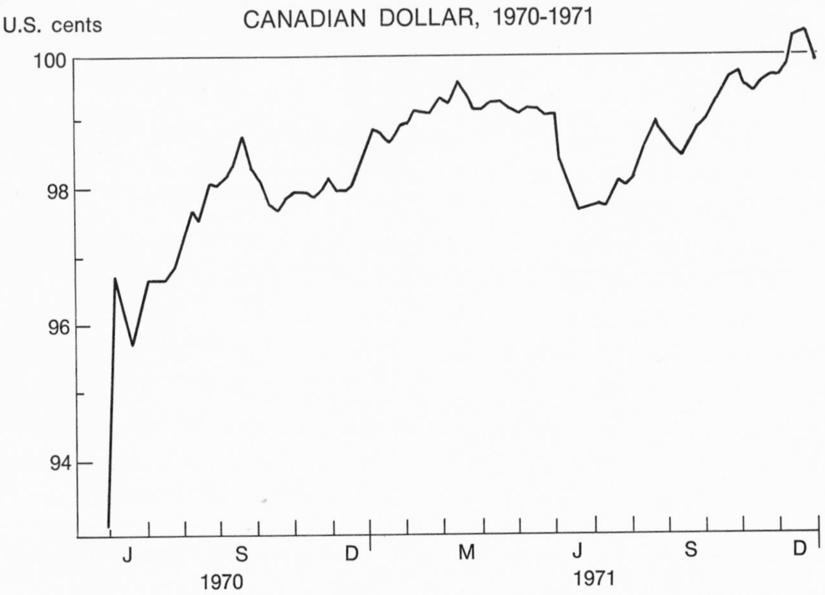

Source: *Bank of Canada Statistical Summary; Bank of Canada Review.*

—$315 million in the first quarter and $226 million in the second (seasonally adjusted; at quarterly, not annual, rates). In addition, there were sizable capital surpluses, with strength coming in the long-term capital sectors in the first quarter (with a surplus of $644 million) and in short-term forms in the second (a surplus of $573 million) [1] as the sustainability of the 92.5¢ par for the Canadian dollar came into question.

The strength of the Canadian current account in the first two quarters of 1970 was entirely due to the greatly improved performance in merchandise trade. In part, the strong performance of the merchandise account was due to more buoyant conditions in overseas markets than in Canada, but this was by no means the sole reason for the size of the trade surplus. Canadian merchandise exports to the United States in the first half of 1970 ran 9.7 percent above their year-earlier level, while imports rose only 2.6 percent. The effects of the U.S.-Canadian automotive agreement of 1965 continued to show

---

[1] The capital account figures are not published in a seasonally adjusted form, presumably because their great quarter-to-quarter variability would raise questions about their meaning.

strongly.[2] U.S. first-half exports to Canada in this sector were unchanged at $1.41 billion between 1969 and 1970, while imports from Canada rose from $1.69 billion to $1.91 billion. The overall bilateral merchandise account moved from approximate balance to a Canadian surplus of $357 million.[3] And this occurred in spite of the weakness in the U.S. economy—between the last quarter of 1969 and the second quarter of 1970, U.S. seasonally adjusted nominal GNP rose at an annual rate of 4.3 percent, while real GNP declined at an annual rate of 1.2 percent. Canada's nominal GNP increased at a 7.0 percent rate, and real GNP increased at a 1.7 percent rate.

Exchange Flexibility and Canadian Domestic Policies

At first glance, the decision of the Canadian government to allow their currency to appreciate might seem paradoxical during a period of high unemployment (over 6 percent, seasonally adjusted). The apparent paradox is, however, attributable to the sharp dilemma in which the government had found itself: inflation and unemployment had coexisted as major problems since 1967. Neither expansion nor contraction was clearly called for by the state of the economy, and to choose a policy was to pick a way between conflicting considerations.

In early 1970, a relaxation was considered in order. In the March budget, a reduction was foreseen in the surplus from $570 million in the previous fiscal year to $130 million in the upcoming year (on a national accounts basis; actual surplus, not full employment surplus; compare Figure 5). The reduction was to be accompanied by an increase of 13 percent in expenditures over the previous year. This stimulus was, however, to be partially offset by restrictions on consumer installment credit. On the monetary side, there was a retreat from the tight conditions of mid-1969, roughly paralleling the move-

---

[2] On the automotive agreement, including statistical problems associated with the bilateral trade balance, see Carl E. Beigie, *The Canada-U.S. Automotive Agreement: an Evaluation* (Washington: Canadian-American Committee [National Planning Association], 1970); the U.S. Government's Annual Reports on the Operation of the Automotive Agreement; and Paul Wonnacott, *The U.S.-Canadian Automotive Agreement: The Early Results* (College Park, Maryland: Bureau of Business and Economic Research, University of Maryland, 1968).

[3] With the exception of the auto data, taken from the *Survey of Current Business*, the trade figures above are taken from Canadian sources. U.S. data show the Canadian bilateral surplus at a higher figure. For all of 1970, for example, Canadian data show a bilateral merchandise surplus of $1.14 billion (Canadian); the U.S. figure is $1.68 billion.

ment in the United States. Following the reduction in the money supply which had occurred in the third quarter of 1969, there were moderate increases in the last quarter of 1969 and the first quarter of 1970 (Figure 7). During the first quarter, Canadian interest rates declined from their early-1970 peaks.

Thus, the decision to allow the Canadian dollar to float at the beginning of June should not be interpreted as part of a sharp restriction on the Canadian economy; rather, it was dictated by a desire to avoid the necessity of moving to a more expansionary policy than was considered appropriate. To be sure, the increase in the value of the Canadian dollar could be expected to have a restrictive effect on the economy (by encouraging imports and discouraging exports, although in the event the Canadian merchandise balance has held up remarkably well). In order to maintain the same general overall posture, therefore, simultaneous steps were taken to offset the direct restraint that would otherwise be produced by the altered exchange rate. The intention of the government not to use the rise in the exchange rate as the basis for a generally restrictive policy was made quite explicit by Finance Minister Benson:

> I advised the [federal-provincial] conference that we fully recognized that any appreciation of the Canadian dollar for an extended period of time would tend to add a further measure of restraint to the economy. I said that further restraint would not be appropriate and that we would offset by other measures any such restraining effects on the economy.[4]

At the time of the float, the finance minister announced that he would not proceed with the restrictions on consumer credit proposed in the March budget. The expenditures side of fiscal policy was further eased, particularly in the case of federal government transfers to the provinces. The bank rate, which had been shaved by ½ percent on May 12, was lowered by another ½ percent to 7 percent on June 1.

Rather than representing a shift in overall policy, then, the floating of the exchange rate represented a change in the policy mix—a change necessitated by the very strong balance of payments, and, in particular, the strong merchandise account. Like any change in the mix, it tended to have differential effects on various parts of the economy.

---

[4] E. J. Benson, Report to the House of Commons on the Federal-Provincial Conference in Winnipeg, June 8, 1970 (mimeographed).

Figure 9

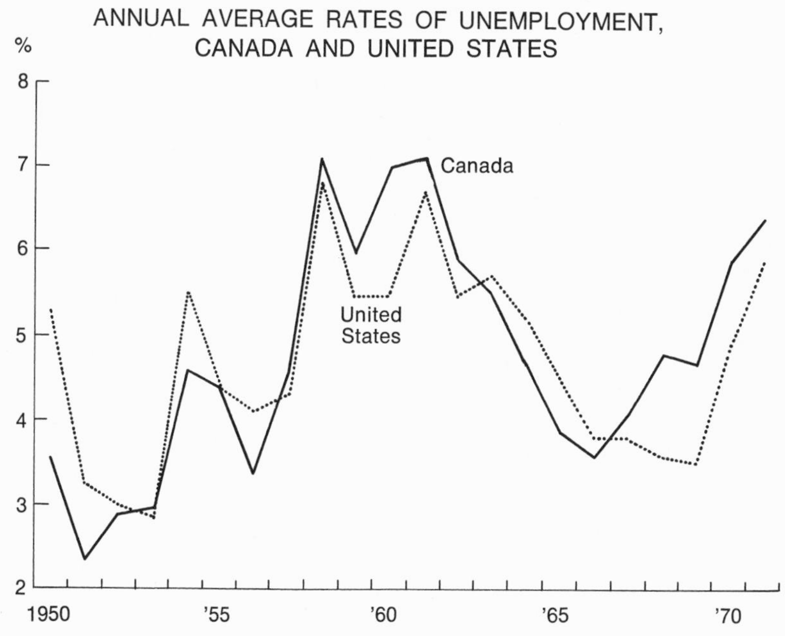

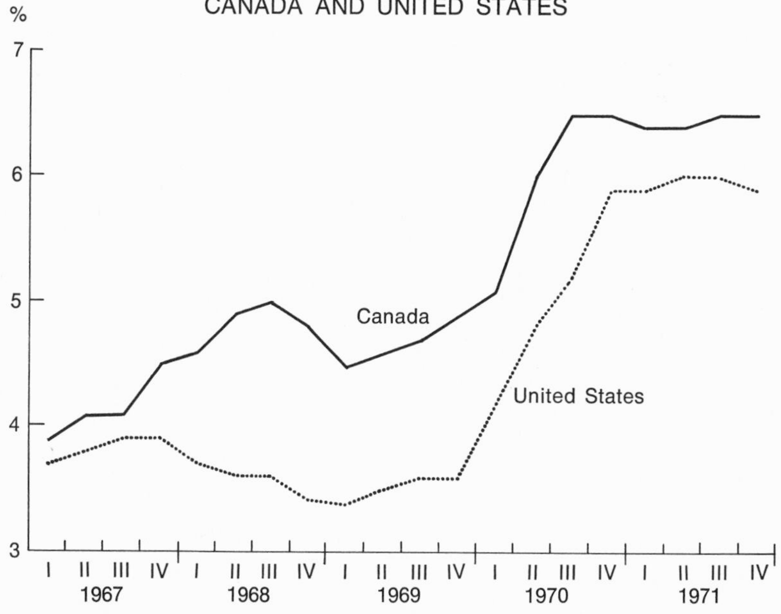

* Seasonally adjusted.

Source: Bank of Canada Review; *Survey of Current Business.*

Figure 10

CONSUMER PRICE INDEXES,
CANADA AND UNITED STATES
(1967=100)
(Quarterly)

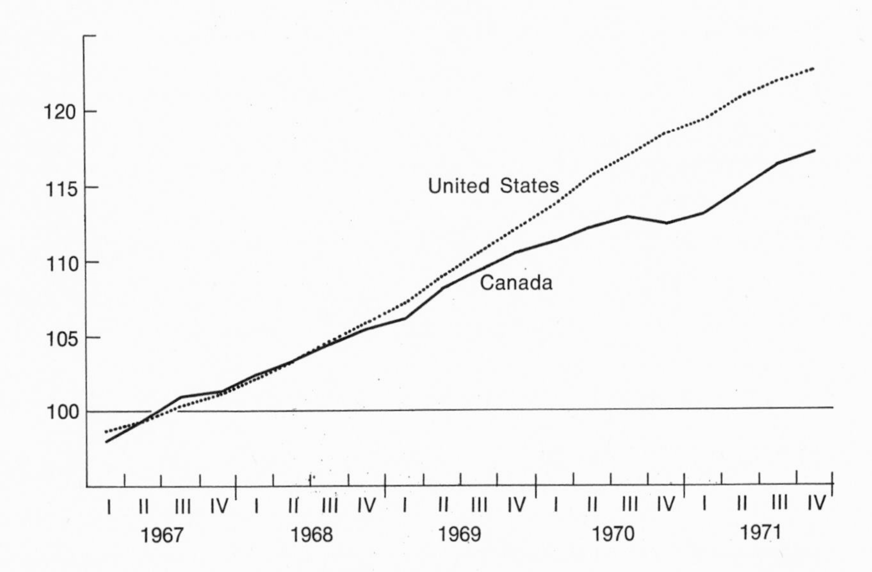

These differential effects are important for two major reasons, both of them connected with the unemployment-inflation dilemma and the possibilities of loosening the bind created for the policy makers. These are (a) the location of the impact on the economy (the "generality" argument) and (b) the double effect of exchange appreciation in restraining inflation.

Generality. The degree of unemployment which will be created by anti-inflationary policies depends to some extent on how general the policies are; where policies hit a narrow sector of the economy, the dislocations will be relatively large. In this respect, an upward movement of the exchange rate can be considered a complement to monetary restraint. An upward adjustment of the Canadian dollar had its primary restraining effect on the producers of exports and import-competing goods: these were, generally speaking, large business organizations, which were less likely to be hit by tight money than some other segments of the economy, and, in particular, the housing market. If policies are to be generally applied, the change in the exchange rate must of course be moderate so that the restraint on export and import-competing industries does not greatly exceed restraint on other segments of the economy. And, indeed, the government and central bank took steps to restrain the extent of the appreciation of the Canadian dollar (see the following section).

A second complication in the "generality" argument is that the restrictive effects of the change in the exchange rate were not coincident with restrictive monetary policies: indeed, they took place at a time when monetary policy was becoming noticeably less restrictive following the rigors of 1969. In passing, it might be noted, however, that some of the sectoral effects of the tight money during 1969 had shown considerable lag—the number of housing starts, which had been 263,300 on a seasonally adjusted annual basis in the first quarter of 1969, dropped throughout 1969 and into the second quarter of 1970, when it amounted to only 139,000 units: the low point in actual construction was naturally further lagged (by one quarter), and in completions, one additional quarter.

The double effect. The second "special" impact of exchange rate appreciation involves the double effect which it has in restraining prices. There is a reduction of aggregate demand, with imports tending to rise and exports tending to be depressed (although this did not show up strongly in the early Canadian figures). This aggregate demand effect, which will be magnified by a multiplier-type process, is the one stressed in theoretical discussions of exchange adjustments. But, exchange rate adjustments may also have a more direct effect in modifying the rate of inflation: because of the competition from lower-priced goods on the world markets, price increases may be directly restrained. In other words, an appreciation of the exchange rate may reduce inflation both by reducing aggregate demand, and by directly influencing pricing decisions in the face of reduced prices of internationally traded goods. A similar argument, it may be noted in passing, may be applied to reductions in tariffs, and, indeed, the Canadian government had at an earlier stage accelerated the Kennedy-Round tariff cuts as an anti-inflationary move.

Insofar as this direct price effect of exchange rate adjustments is important, it can have the happy result of reducing the inflation-unemployment dilemma. With the direct effect on prices, the degree of inflation associated with any particular level of aggregate demand will be reduced.

The relatively low rate of increase of prices in Canada during 1970 may be evidence of this direct price effect. In the three previous years, the price-unemployment dilemma had been getting worse in Canada, but in 1970, there was a movement back towards the his-

Figure 11

PRICE PERFORMANCE
AND UNEMPLOYMENT
CANADA, 1962-1970

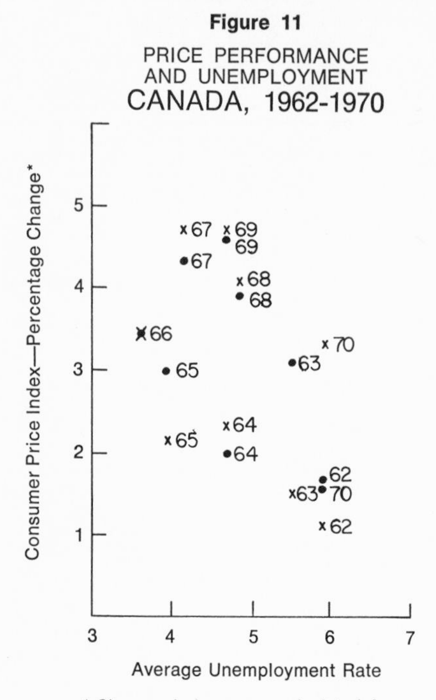

* Change during year, calculated from end of year indexes (derived by averaging December of a given year with January of subsequent year).

• Total CPI.

x CPI excluding food.

Figure 12

PRICE PERFORMANCE
AND UNEMPLOYMENT
UNITED STATES, 1962-1970

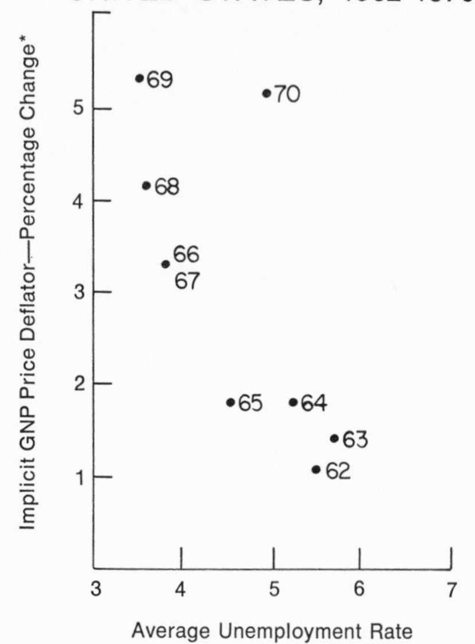

* Change during year, calculated from end of year indexes (derived by averaging fourth quarter of a given year with first quarter of subsequent year).

torical relationships (Figure 11). This was in notable contrast to the United States, where the dilemma appeared about this time following the earlier declines in the unemployment rate (Figure 12).

Unfortunately, however, these aggregate data do not by themselves demonstrate the strength of the mitigating effects of the exchange rate change on the price-unemployment dilemma. Much of the price improvement was in the food sector, where the concentrations of market power associated with the price-unemployment dilemma tend to be weak. Nevertheless, even if the food sector is excluded, there was still a welcome reduction in the rate of inflation. (The consumer price indexes are used for Canada in Figure 11 in order to highlight the different paths of food and other products.) But, with the exclusion of food, the reduction of the rate of inflation which occurred in 1970 did not clearly involve a mitigation of the price-unemployment dilemma: the 1970 point, with higher unemployment than in 1969, lies closer to the unfavorable 1967-69 trade-off than it does to the more favorable 1962-66 relationship. In spite of this ambiguity, however, there is some evidence of an exchange rate effect on non-food prices. In the months immediately following the upward float of the Canadian dollar, the rate of price increase was particularly low—at an annual rate of 2.1 percent from May to September (excluding food), compared to 3.3 percent for the year as a whole.

But, to complicate matters further, there were at least two factors other than the exchange appreciation which may have contributed to the reduction of the rate of inflation in 1970. First, since 1966, Canada had had excess capacity, which exerted an anti-inflationary force on the economy. Second, the Prices and Incomes Commission (PIC) had had some success in early 1970 in getting businessmen to agree to price increases which were less than adequate to make up for rising costs, although on the other hand the PIC had been notably unsuccessful in gaining the cooperation of labor. The difficulties of separating the effects of the PIC and the exchange appreciation are compounded by the approximate coincidence of the breakdown of the price agreements and the end of the upward movement of the Canadian dollar in early 1971.[5] And, indeed, there have been signs of a renewal of high rates of inflation in 1971 after the comparative respite of 1970.

More direct evidence on the relationship between the exchange rate and the rate of inflation suggests that the 5 percent increase in the value of the Canadian dollar between May and August of 1970 may have had a direct restraining influence on the Canadian consumer price index somewhere in the range of ½ to 1 percent (excluding any indirect effects through the level of aggregate demand). The recent econometric work of the Bank of Canada—model RDX2[6]—finds a foreign influence in three of the four consumer price series studied—to wit, motor vehicles, other durables, and nondurables and semidurables. (The service component of the consumer price index, comprising 18 percent of the non-food index, is constructed primarily from wage rate data by the Bureau of Statistics, and wage rates naturally enough provide the explanation for service prices in RDX2.) The nondurables and semidurables (42 percent weight) have an elasticity with respect to the import price of 0.10: that is, a 1 percent change in import prices would lead to a 0.1 percent change in domestic prices of this category. For durables (16 percent),[7] the "other durable"

[5] For a brief review of the activities of the PIC, see Eric Schiff, *Income Policies Abroad* (Washington: American Enterprise Institute for Public Policy Research, April 1971), pp. 35-42. Schiff concluded (p. 41) that it was diffcult to tell how much of Canada's improved price performance in 1970 was due to market conditions, especially the exchange appreciation, and how much was due to the restraint program of the PIC.

[6] Bank of Canada, December 1970 (mimeographed).

[7] The weights shown add to less than 100 percent; the RDX2 equations do not cover all components of the consumer price index.

category shows the most easily quantifiable effect of foreign prices. The elasticity of this index is 0.27 with respect to the U.S. consumer durable price multiplied by the exchange rate; a change in the exchange rate will have an effect about one quarter as large on this component of the price index.

This approach does not delve into the question of whether the Canadian prices of goods imported from the United States might fail to reflect changes in the exchange rate. This point was addressed by Robert M. Dunn in an article entitled "Flexible Exchange Rates and Oligopoly Pricing: A Study of Canadian Markets." [8] Dunn presented evidence that, in the oligopolistic areas of window glass, gasoline, crude oil, rolling-mill products, copper, and coal, "changes in the relationship between Canadian and U.S. prices . . . were not determined or even influenced by changes in flexible exchange rates" between 1950 and 1962. However, the basic issue that Dunn was getting at was quite different from our question of whether a one-way appreciation of the Canadian dollar would, over a period of several quarters, result in a reduction in the rate of inflation; rather, Dunn was concerned with testing Ronald McKinnon's contention that flexible exchange rates would cause day-to-day shifts in domestic prices as exchange rates fluctuate. Thus, Dunn looked only at simultaneous and one-quarter lagged data. He concluded that it was plausible for oligopolistic industries to keep their domestic prices fixed in response to short-term fluctuations in the exchange rate.

Dunn's conclusions do not severely undercut mine for several reasons. First, insofar as exchange rate appreciation may be aimed at (or result in) less rapid upward movements of prices rather than actual downward price adjustments, any oligopolistic tendency towards stickiness of prices would tend to fortify rather than undercut the anti-inflationary effects of exchange rate changes. Second, it may well be that oligopolistic industries average over an extended period of a year or so; that is, they do not respond to temporary fluctuations around a given exchange rate, but do respond periodically (but not necessarily within one quarter) to significant one-way adjustments of the exchange rate. This might be particularly true of an oligopoly which extends over both countries. (Compare the discussion below of automobile pricing.)

The automobile sector showed a strong foreign influence, but one not easily reducible to an elasticity coefficient, since the automotive agreement of 1965 constituted the major international influence.

---

[8] *Journal of Political Economy*, January 1970, pp. 140-51.

However, if we turn to other, admittedly fragmentary, data on automobile pricing in Canada there is good reason to believe that the exchange rate adjustment did significantly influence pricing decisions for Canadian cars for the new model year beginning in late 1970. Following the auto pact, there was a reduction in Canadian-U.S. price differentials (exclusive of taxes, dealer markups, etc.) from approximately 9 or 10 percent in the mid-sixties to about 5 to 6 percent in the 1969 model year, but then the rate of decrease tended to level off, with little change in the differential for the 1970 model year. By the time of the introduction of the 1971 cars, the Canadian dollar had appreciated about 5 percent, and about four-fifths of this showed up in reduced increases in Canadian car prices. That is, if no adjustment is made in the calculations for the change in the exchange rate, the Canadian-U.S. price differential fell to somewhere in the neighborhood of 1 to 2 percent, or, put somewhat differently, following the 5 percent exchange rate adjustment, Canadian car prices in Canadian dollars went up for the new model year by about 4 percent less than U.S. car prices went up in U.S. dollar terms.

While there is more than one explanation which may be offered for this observation—in particular, pricing decisions for Canadian automobiles may have been influenced by U.S. congressional complaints regarding the continuing price gap and the failure of the Canadians to move to complete free trade in automotive products originating in the United States—the price data are consistent with the hypothesis that substantially all the exchange rate increase was reflected in lower rates of price increases in Canada. Indeed, given the fact that pricing decisions are made for a year's span, and given the pronounced view by the Canadian government that the Canadian dollar was showing unusual strength, it is possible to argue that the lower price increase in Canada fully reflected the expected average appreciation for the 1971-72 car year, over the 92.5¢ base.

To summarize existing evidence on the relationship between the 5 percent appreciation of the Canadian dollar in mid-1970 and the consumer price index exclusive of food: it would appear there was no direct effect on the service component (18 percent of the total); there was a lowering of the nondurables and semidurables (42 percent weight) about one tenth as great as the change in the exchange rate; and there was a reduction in the durable sector (16 percent) at least a quarter as great as the exchange appreciation, and perhaps substantially more, depending on how automobile pricing is interpreted. This gives a minimum effect on the price index of about 0.5 percent resulting from the 5 percent change in the exchange rate. In this way, the appreciation of the Canadian dollar contributed to—but was by no means solely responsible for—the moderation of the rate of inflation during 1970. The appreciation of the Canadian currency both made a direct contribution to the easing of inflation, and permitted monetary policy to remain on a less expansive course than would have been required if the 92.5¢ peg had been maintained.

The Objectives of Canadian Exchange Rate Policy

From the very beginning of the float in 1970, the Canadian authorities stressed that they did not intend to let the exchange rate adjust completely to market forces: efforts would be made to keep the Canadian dollar from rising too quickly. In explaining the decision to float, Finance Minister Benson on June 1 stated:

> Lower prices in Canada for imported goods will be of assistance in moderating the upward trend of costs and prices. Any appreciation of the Canadian dollar for any extended period of time, without offsetting measures, would however tend to have further restraining effect on the economy. This would not be appropriate in present circumstances. The Exchange Fund will therefore stand ready to maintain orderly conditions in the exchange market and to operate for the time being to moderate any appreciation of the Canadian dollar.[9]

In a longer term context, a similar point was made by the governor of the Bank of Canada:

> The exchange rate is a very important price in a country that trades with the outside world on the scale that Canada does: changes in it have important effects on the level and nature of economic activity in Canada, particularly on the position of industries that export and that compete with imports. It is not therefore possible to ignore it, even when it floats. Public financial management must continue to be concerned that the exchange rate is broadly suitable to the development of Canada's international trade, and compatible with the desired structure of our balance of payments, in particular the size of the balance on current account. . . . If the exchange rate moves or threatens to move outside that range it will be prudent to review the mix of financial policy in Canada to see if some other mix would be more appropriate. Whether it will be monetary policy or fiscal policy or both

[9] Hon. E. J. Benson, Statement on the Par Value of the Canadian Dollar, June 1, 1970 (mimeographed).

that will need to be changed will depend on the circumstances.[10]

The exchange rate should not be allowed to change too much, or the internationally trading sectors of the economy will be hard hit.[11] This line of argument touches the point made earlier, that a degree of restrictiveness exerted through exchange appreciation may contribute to the generality of economic policies, and therefore reduce the overall pain resulting from any particular level of restriction—provided that the exchange appreciation is limited.

In spite of the overall strength of Canadian exports, a number of important export sectors found their profit positions squeezed by the appreciation of the Canadian dollar. Most vocal, perhaps, was the paper and forestry industry, which suffered a major reduction in profits with the appreciation of the Canadian dollar—$39 million in net profits in the last two quarters of 1970, compared to $108 million in the similar period a year earlier.[12] A question arises as to how much of this reduction was the result of the exchange rate and how much the result of the effects of the U.S. slowdown in advertising; in any case, the appreciation of the Canadian dollar clearly made the situation more difficult for this industry and others heavily engaged in trade.[13] Following the weak profit reports in early 1971, a financial

---

[10] Bank of Canada, *Annual Report*, 1970, pp. 9-10.

[11] This point was also made very explicitly by Mr. Rasminsky in his April 28, 1971, speech to the Canadian Club of Vancouver (mimeographed):

> The exchange rate . . . is far too important a price in the economic life of a trading nation to be ignored. I hardly need remind British Columbians of the problems which a considerable appreciation of the exchange rate can create for major export industries.

[12] Dominion Bureau of Statistics, *Industrial Corporations, Financial Statistics*, IV, 1970, p. 53.

[13] Professor Harry Johnson expressed little sympathy for the paper industry's tale of woe, *Proceedings of the Standing Senate Committee on National Finance*, May 26, 1971, p. 31:

> Senator Beaubien: "The second question I want to ask you, Dr. Johnson, is: We have a floating rate now and our dollar has gone up in terms of the American dollar, and the paper industry is just on the borderline as to whether it is going to go bust or not in Canada. If our dollar goes up a little more the chances are rather good that it will go bust. What happens then? Then you have a great deal of unemployment in the industry."
>
> Dr. Johnson: "Senator, I would never take an industry's word on the point at which it will go bust. The paper industry in Canada has been on the verge of going bust ever since I was a school child, but all jobs did not disappear. What happens mostly is that the capital gets revalued. The company may have to go into bankruptcy and take a loss, but we are still exporting paper."

analyst remarked that the Canadian dollar "floats like a butterfly, but, from a profit point of view, it stings like a bee." [14]

Methods used to limit the exchange appreciation: monetary policy. The Canadian government used two methods of keeping down the value of the Canadian dollar: purchases of foreign exchange, and recommendations to borrowers that they use the Canadian capital market rather than New York. These steps were reinforced by the Bank of Canada, which followed a monetary policy designed to keep down Canadian interest rates and thus discourage recourse to the U.S. capital market. The importance of monetary policy in keeping down the exchange value of the Canadian dollar was stressed by Deputy Governor J. R. Beattie of the Bank of Canada:

> Given the public and private demand for funds which has existed, keeping the increase in the money supply appreciably lower would have resulted in higher short term interest rates than those we have experienced. This would have exerted some drag on domestic economic recovery both directly and through encouraging short term capital inflows which would have pushed up our exchange rate further, with consequent discouragement to exports and increase in imports. It will be clear that monetary policy has recently given a high priority to avoiding an exchange rate that was inappropriate to our economic circumstances.[15]

Because of the exchange rate objective, monetary policy thus continued to be subject to external restraints under the flexible exchange rate: the exchange rate objective has meant, in effect, that there is an intermediate situation between a pegged rate and a fully flexible one which moves freely without an official target price. As made clear from Mr. Beattie's statement, however, the external influence has been in the direction which was considered desirable for domestic purposes, that is, toward greater monetary expansion. While there has been an external influence on monetary policy, there has been no conflict between domestic and international objectives of monetary policy.

Exchange fund activity. Between the beginning of the float in June and the end of 1970, Canadian official holdings of convertible foreign

---

[14] *Financial Post*, April 3, 1971, p. 3. See the discussion of Robert M. Dunn, *Canada's Experience with Fixed and Flexible Exchange Rates in a North American Capital Market* (Washington: Canadian-American Committee, National Planning Association, May 1971), p. 73.

[15] J. R. Beattie, Remarks on Monetary Policy to the Outlook Conference of the Conference Board, Toronto, October 7, 1971 (mimeographed).

currencies increased by $493 million. Not all of this, however, can be attributed to market intervention during the June-December period: more than half came from the execution of the $360 million in forward contracts accumulated during the first five months of the year when the Canadian government was attempting to hold the 92.5 percent par. In general, the accumulation of reserves can be interpreted as the exertion of a degree of counterpressure during a period of a generally rising value for the Canadian dollar.[16]

Surprisingly, there was one notable exception to this general pattern of leaning against the wind. During September, when the Canadian dollar moved quickly up to its 1970 peak, the Exchange Fund Account reduced its holdings both of U.S. dollars ($63.1 million) and of U.S. dollar forward contracts ($40.3 million). Unfortunately, day-to-day data are not available. Short-term timing is a matter of some importance because the Canadian dollar ran quickly up 1½¢ to a peak of about 99-11/16 in the third week of September, and then fell off just as quickly by 1½¢ by the end of the month. The overall monthly statistics available suggest that the activity of the authorities may have been destabilizing during this month, as they were buying $103 million worth of Canadian dollars (i.e., selling U.S. dollars) during the month that a peak was reached in the price.[17] This is rather surprising, given the declared desire of the authorities both to stabilize short-term swings and to keep down the value of the Canadian dollar. Unfortunately, this month is skipped over by the 1970 Report on the Exchange Fund Account, which notes simply that "From June to the end of the year, the Exchange Fund Account intervened only occasionally in the exchange market, essentially to maintain orderly conditions in the market when the rate tended to rise or to fall excessively." [18] The puzzle remains unsolved.

The $129 million net increase in the Canadian foreign exchange position ($493 million in currencies less $364 forward) during the June-

---

[16] For simplicity, this analysis slides over the question of whether a neutral exchange fund stance would involve zero changes in Canadian holdings of convertible foreign currencies, or zero changes in total Canadian reserves, including the Canadian position in the International Monetary Fund. (Allocations of Special Drawing Rights should clearly be excluded, and have been excluded from Table 1.) This issue does not substantially affect the points raised in the text.

[17] Presumably the reduction in the forward position simply reflected executions of forward contracts acquired during the early part of the year, and as such did not reflect active policy. However, as such executions would add to U.S. dollar holdings unless equivalent spot sales were made, the total of $103 million is the appropriate measure of "active" Exchange Fund Account intervention.

[18] Department of Finance, Report on the Exchange Fund Account, 1970 (mimeographed), p. 1.

Table 1
CHANGE IN RESERVES AND EXCHANGE RATE CHANGE, JUNE 1970 - AUGUST 1971

	Appreciation of Canadian Dollar[a]		Change in Official Holdings of Convertible Foreign Currencies[b]	Change in Official Reserves[b] (excl. SDR allocations)	Change in Official Holdings of U.S. Forward Dollars[c] (millions)	Total Change in Position[b] (excl. SDR allocations)
1970	Closing rates (¢)	Average noon rates (¢)				
May	− 3/16	0	230.3	261.6	345.3	606.9
June	4.0	3.44	244.4	249.4	−172.9	76.5
July	7/8	0.64	35.6	110.6	− 40.7	69.9
Aug.	3/4	1.06	157.3	171.7	− 55.3	116.4
Sept.	− 1/32	0.55	− 62.7	− 62.7	− 40.3	−103.0
Oct.	− 5/32	−0.55	48.0	53.9	3.4	57.3
Nov.	3/32	0.14	37.1	37.6	− 40.4	− 2.8
Dec.	25/32	0.26	33.2	34.5	− 17.5	17.0
1971						
Jan.	9/32	0.58	2.4	2.4	N.A.	N.A.
Feb.	5/32	0.41	50.7	51.2	N.A.	N.A.
Mar.	− 1/16	0.12	77.8	− 5.6	N.A.	N.A.
April	− 5/32	−0.13	15.9	9.2	N.A.	N.A.
May	− 5/32	−0.11	41.2	24.8	N.A.	N.A.
June	−1 1/4	−1.25	− 21.8	− 26.9	N.A.	N.A.
July	7/16	0.01	73.7	72.0	N.A.	N.A.
Aug.	5/16	0.78	262.2	68.4	N.A.	N.A.
Sept.	21/32	0.04	− 11.6	− 0.6	N.A.	N.A.
Oct.	3/8	0.85	71.5	79.9	N.A.	N.A.
Nov.	7/32	0.07	194.1	202.1	N.A.	N.A.
Dec.	3/32	0.45	281.5	296.8	N.A.	N.A.

[a] Change in price of U.S.$ in Canada, with sign changed. [b] In millions of U.S.$.
[c] Exchange Fund Account and Bank of Canada.
Sources: Bank of Canada, *Statistical Review;* Minister of Finance, *Report on Exchange Fund Account,* 1970. (Mimeographed.)

December period represented a moderate activity on the part of the Exchange Fund Account to keep down the level of the Canadian dollar. To put it in quantitative terms, it amounted to about a sixth of the very large increase of the first five months which had pushed the dollar from its peg. Apart from the unexplained activity in September, the operations of the Exchange Fund Account seem to have been more directed at keeping the Canadian dollar down than at stabilizing the rate during the last seven months of 1970. In particular, the accumulation of $57 million during October contributed to the fall in the price of the Canadian dollar on the exchanges. During 1971, the picture was less clear and less complete. Accumulations—February, July, August, October, and November—were made in the face of upward movements in the Canadian dollar, and therefore can be interpreted as the result of a desire to stabilize rather than to push the Canadian dollar down. The size of the foreign currency acquisition in November —$194 million—indicates a strong effort on the part of the Canadian authorities to keep their dollar from rising above the U.S. dollar.

The overall impression that the Canadian authorities were engaged in stabilizing activity is fortified by the reduction in reserves in June, which moderated the sharpest downward slide of the dollar to date. Indeed, during June and July, the changes in reserves indicate that the fund was performing a classical stabilizing operation. During June, speculative pressures built up against the Canadian dollar in the face of uncertainty over the June budget and tax reform message, and in July there was a rebound as traders covered their forward contracts.[19] The purchase of Canadian dollars by the Exchange Fund Account in June and the purchase of U.S. dollars in July acted to slow down the fall in the Canadian dollar in June and its rebound in July. The only notable evidence on the other side is the $41 million accumulation of currencies in May which added to the downward pressures on the Canadian currency during that month.

Exhortations to borrowers. From the beginning of the period of the float, the Canadian authorities have exhorted borrowers to use Canadian rather than U.S. capital markets as a way of keeping down the value of the Canadian dollar. Both the minister of finance and the governor of the Bank of Canada asked Canadian borrowers to explore very carefully the possibilities of financing in the Canadian market before going to foreign capital markets.[20] This request was given force

---

[19] Frederic Waganiere, "Money Markets," *Financial Post*, July 31, 1971, p. 15.

[20] Bank of Canada, *Annual Report*, 1970, p. 7.

by the changing state of the Canadian capital market, where conditions were becoming significantly easier. During the spring and summer of 1970, Canadian-U.S. interest rate differentials generally moved in favor of the Canadian borrower, with yields on shorter term government bonds (three to five years) in Canada falling below U.S. rates. By the first quarter of 1971, however, foreign borrowing by provinces showed signs of revival, rising to $197 million from the low rate of $18 million in the last quarter of 1970. With the upward movement of Canadian interest rates in the second quarter of 1971 (both absolutely, and, to a much lesser extent, compared to U.S. yields), the minister of finance strongly repeated his request that borrowers look to the Canadian market. In a letter to investment dealers and provincial treasurers and finance ministers, Mr. Benson wrote:

> Last year Canada achieved a substantial current account surplus. . . . The favorable trade balance has been of great benefit in contributing to the strength of the economy. This situation carries with it, however, the need to bring about a corresponding adjustment to the net inflows of capital into Canada. . . . I am continuing to urge Canadians to hold their borrowing in foreign markets to a minimum. . . . It is because of the recent increase in Canadian borrowing abroad that I am writing to . . . request that the maximum possible use be made of the Canadian capital market and that foreign borrowing be kept to the absolute minimum.
>
> I firmly believe that . . . limiting foreign borrowing will benefit all Canadians by contributing directly to greater production and employment in Canada.[21]

The combination of moral suasion and easier conditions in the Canadian financial markets from the second quarter of 1970 to the first quarter of 1971 resulted in a major decline in Canadian foreign borrowing. In those four quarters, total Canadian new issues in foreign markets were $1,012 million (Canadian), compared to $1,986 million in the same four quarters one year earlier. Net of retirements, the decline was from $1,587 million to $536 million. During the first nine months of 1971, net new issues of Canadian securities payable in foreign currency ran at an annual rate of only $350 million, compared to $650 million in 1970, and $1,700 million in 1969.

[21] Department of Finance, *News Release*, April 23, 1971. Bank of Canada Governor Louis Rasminsky made a similar request: "I regard it as very much in the national interest that all borrowers . . . do as much of their financing in Canada as it is feasible for them to do." Louis Rasminsky, Remarks before a meeting of the Canadian Club of Vancouver, April 28, 1971 (mimeographed).

6
STANDARDS OF GOOD BEHAVIOR: AN UNSOLVED PROBLEM

Exchange Flexibility and Standards of Good Behavior

During the past year and a half, Canadian exchange rate policy has been developed with the needs of the domestic economy in mind. In early 1970, the Canadian dollar was allowed to float upward in order to avoid the degree of monetary expansion which would have been necessary to maintain the pegged rate of 92.5¢. This did not, however, signal an abrupt shift towards restriction, but rather was a way of responding to the balance of payments pressures created by very strong merchandise trade developments. Expansive domestic policies were then able to proceed in a measured manner, with the exchange rate adjustment reducing immediate inflationary problems and mitigating the unemployment-inflation dilemma. In order to prevent further pressures on industries heavily engaged in international trade, the government resisted upward movement of the currency, thereby reaching a compromise between a fully flexible exchange rate and the maintenance of a fixed par.

Because it represented a middle-of-the-road position, a rather strong *a priori* case can be made that Canadian exchange rate policy met reasonable standards of good international behavior. The strong advocate of fixed exchange rates would naturally dissent from this conclusion, on the grounds that the Canadian experiment with exchange rate flexibility in itself indicated that Canada was falling short on her obligations to the international monetary system. And, indeed, Canada did come in for some criticism on these grounds. But, given the increasing frequency of exchange rate flexibility, it is in my view less important to rehash the old question of responsibility to a fixed exchange rate system, than it is to consider what standards of good behavior should be applied to countries with flexible exchange rates, and to consider what light the Canadian experience sheds on such standards.

There are questions regarding what standards might be applied to exchange fund operations, what standards to monetary policies aimed at influencing the exchange rate, and what standards to moral suasion such as that used by Canada to discourage borrowing in the United States. The Canadian view is that it is desirable to keep out (debt) capital, and thereby keep down the price of the Canadian dollar, stimulate exports, and increase employment. This may look from other countries to be painfully close to the attempts during the 1930s to push off unemployment problems on other countries. Although the magnitude of the problem is dramatically smaller than it was in the thirties, it is nevertheless important to look for standards of international conduct.

The difficulty of the problem is underlined by the changes which have recently been taking place in U.S. attitudes on appropriate exchange rate policy. Following the German float in May of 1971, the U.S. government was hesitant about endorsing upward movements of exchange rates as an anti-inflationary tool. In late May, Secretary Connally observed that:

> . . . the question of codifying a degree of additional flexibility with regard to exchange rate practices is clearly relevant. . . .
>
> The danger is plain. To revert to the use of exchange rates as a supplementary tool of domestic policy is fraught with danger to the essential stability and sustainability of the system as a whole.[1]

These reservations about exchange appreciation,[2] even in the face of strong upward market pressures on the mark, were soon superseded by the insistence of President Nixon in his August 15 address that countries with unfair exchange rates revalue, and the backing up of this request with the import surcharge. In his September 30 speech to the IMF-IBRD meetings, Secretary Connally declared that the United States would be prepared to remove the surcharge

---

[1] Remarks of the Hon. John B. Connally at the International Banking Conference of the American Bankers Association, Munich, Germany, May 28, 1971, Treasury Department News Release (mimeographed).

[2] There were reports of stronger private U.S. opposition to the upward German float. In the *Wall Street Journal,* May 26, 1971, Richard Janssen quotes a U.S. government official at the conference as complaining privately

> that Germany isn't "playing the rules of the game," arguing that Bonn is deliberately using its exchange rate policy to influence its domestic economy.

if other governments will make tangible progress towards dismantling specific barriers to trade over coming weeks and will be prepared to allow market realities freely to determine exchange rates for their currencies for a transitional period.[3]

Unfortunately, while some principles of good behavior do suggest themselves, the problem of standards turns out to be a knotty one, and some of these questions remain unsolved in the discussion below: we are left in the position of recommending further study.

Concern regarding an international code of behavior was particularly strong in the immediate postwar period, when memories of protection and competitive devaluations during the depression led to stressing the prevention of competitive exchange rate changes through the International Monetary Fund arrangements, and to the General Agreement on Tariffs and Trade. Essentially, of course, the concern is that a single country, in an effort to deal with domestic problems, will take steps which cause significant harm to its trading partners.

Tariffs, monetary policy, and exchange market intervention. One criterion which may be suggested to distinguish acceptable behavior is the probable overall effect if trading partners respond in kind. It is this which makes the use of tariffs such a problematical way of dealing with unemployment: if other countries respond in kind, the improvement in the trade balance and the overall stimulation will tend to be cancelled out. There will be a general decline in efficiency because of the strangling of trade, and also, quite possibly, a reduction in the overall level of employment because of the general disruption of economic activities related to international trade.

At the other end of the spectrum is monetary expansion, which, under a system of flexible exchange rates, will operate through a repelling of capital, a depreciation in the exchange rate, and thereby an increase in exports and a decrease in imports. At first glance, this might seem to be quite similar to the use of tariffs, since the international side of the economy is seen as contributing to the reduction in unemployment. But the potential international destructiveness of such policies is quite different from the destructiveness of the use of tariffs. Expansive monetary policies may have depressing effects on trading partners because of the depreciation of the exchange rate, but there will be some offsetting effects. These come in the form

---

[3] International Monetary Fund, *Summary Proceedings, Annual Meeting,* 1971, p. 219.

of the import stimulation resulting from domestic expansion (although this will tend to be offset by a further depreciation of the exchange rate if it is freely flexible), and through the expansive interest rate effects of the capital inflow (although this will depend in part on the monetary policy response in the partner country). But, more important, if trading partners respond in kind through monetary expansion of their own, the exchange rate effects will tend to cancel out, but there will be an overall expansion of demand and employment in the world economy. Thus, in contrast to tariff increases as a means of stimulating employment, against which a *prima facie* case exists from the viewpoint of the international community, the use of domestic monetary policies may be considered intrinsically legitimate.

Somewhere in the middle lies the use of exchange fund operations to depress the value of the currency. A response in kind by foreign partners will offset the exchange rate and trade effects of the intervention, and should, theoretically, leave the situation basically unchanged. In practice, however, there may be major problems for the United States because of the use of the dollar as an intervention currency and because of the inhibitions on U.S. foreign exchange operations (see below).

One general argument for and one general argument against the use of exchange fund operations may be noted. Insofar as other countries are in a different cyclical position, the depression of a country's currency may work to the common good by stimulating activity in the depressed economy and restraining it in the inflating country. Indeed, this argument may be more broadly applicable than simply to "cyclical" conditions. While the case is clear that a rise in the exchange rate was in Germany's interest in 1969 in order to restrain an overly buoyant economy, it can also be argued—and was indeed argued above—that the rise of the Canadian dollar in 1970 was in the Canadian domestic interest in spite of the level of unemployment. Because it acted directly in restraining prices and was accompanied by monetary and fiscal expansion, the Canadian appreciation temporarily softened the unemployment-inflation dilemma. In the case of both Germany and Canada, the appreciations were the result of market forces rather than fund intervention, but the point regarding the relationship between domestic conditions and the exchange rate is nonetheless relevant.

On the other hand, competing attempts by two countries to push their exchange rate in opposite directions may create a general atmosphere of friction, even though the actions themselves are neutral—that is, they cancel one another out. On a general level we are left with an ambiguous view as to the international acceptability of exchange fund operations aimed at changing the exchange rate in line with the needs of the domestic economy. This matter is worth pursuing: unfortunately, it gets messier still.

Exchange Fund Operations: A More Detailed Look

Upward vs. downward pressures. The discussion above has made no specific distinction between the use of market intervention to appreciate the home currency and its use to depreciate that currency; depending on the circumstances, either might contribute to the smooth operation of the domestic economy. Yet attitudes towards exchange appreciation and exchange depreciation are clearly uneven in strength: given the general desires for strong current account balances, actions to depress the home currency are much more likely to lead to foreign resentment than are actions which increase its value. In addition, any rise in the home currency for domestic reasons tends to be self-limiting in a way that depreciations are not, since the industries engaged in international trade will object to a large appreciation. Some rise in the exchange rate could have been considered a contribution to the domestic economy in Canada in 1970; but the government stressed from the start that it would be against a really large appreciation. Thus, in spite of minor rumblings against the German upward float in May (which, again, was due to market forces rather than official intervention), the problem is basically one-sided. Questions of international criteria arise where countries with flexible exchanges accumulate reserves,[4] but decreases in reserves can pretty well be ignored.

While purchases of Canadian dollars by the Exchange Fund Account during September 1970 were puzzling (since the Canadian dollar reached a peak that month), they were nothing for other countries to get excited about. (To reiterate the caution regarding the September intervention by the Exchange Fund Account: conclusions must be tentative, because only month-end reserve data are available. It is possible that the reserve decrease of September 1970 occurred entirely after the peak in the Canadian dollar was reached, and slowed down the drop from the peak rather than contributing to its

[4] Special Drawing Rights allocations are a clear exception, arising as they do from the creation of reserve assets deemed necessary in a world of expanding international transactions, and being acquired without market intervention.

height.) On the other hand, the actions of the Exchange Fund Account in June 1961 and October 1970, which pushed down a declining Canadian dollar, constituted the type of action which is potentially dangerous, although in these cases it was modest in scope ($36 million and $48 million, with some of this being offset in the forward market in the 1961 instance) and limited in duration (in July, August and September of 1961 reserve holdings declined; between November 1970 and February 1971, the Canadian dollar rose).

The principle that countries should refrain from exchange accumulations as a means of exchange depreciation is a good starting point in the search for standards of good behavior. Unfortunately, as will be seen below, international interrelations are sufficiently complex that any simple criterion is inadequate.

Resistance to market pressures on the exchanges. The use of an exchange fund to push down a declining rate is the most questionable type of fund intervention: a much more nebulous problem arises when the exchange fund acquires reserves in order to prevent the exchange rate of the home currency from rising. (This category includes most of the Canadian intervention since the beginning of the float in June 1970.) Pegged exchange rates are certainly a legitimate alternative to flexible rates, and exchange fund operations which resist movements of a flexible rate and thereby reduce the amplitude of fluctuation can be considered a compromise between a pegged rate and a freely flexible one. The question might be raised, however, as to whether a country which resists an upward movement of its exchange rate acquires any obligation also to resist downward movements to an equal degree, in order to avoid a downward bias. There is a second justification for accumulating reserves as the currency appreciates. Exports and imports take time to adjust to a changed exchange rate, and the degree of appreciation (or depreciation) in the face of a balance of payments disturbance may be greater in the short run than is necessary for adjustment to the disturbance over the long run.

With the close communications and rapid transportation between the U.S. and Canadian markets, it might seem that responses of trade flows to changes in the exchange rate between Canada and the U.S. should be more rapid than is generally the case in international trade. However, close connections do not necessarily speed response: they may slow it, particularly where the close connection has led to integration within industries. In particular, the integration within the automobile industry as a result of the automotive agreement of 1965 has resulted not only in a great increase in trade—with motor vehicles and parts constituting about 30 percent of total Canadian exports to the United States—but also in a slowness of response. Because of the lags in parts procurement and the brief time span between the June float and the beginning of production of the 1971 models, the effects of the Canadian appreciation will not show up substantially until data for the last third of 1971 become available.[5]

Capital flows and the provinces. One of the difficulties in trying to develop criteria for exchange fund operations is that there are indirect ways of doing quite similar things without official intervention in the exchange market. During the Canadian float, government and central bank exhortations for provinces and other borrowers to use the Canadian capital market tended to keep down the price of the Canadian dollar without exchange market operations. Indeed, the decline of Canadian net foreign long-term borrowing between the beginning of the float and the end of the first quarter of 1971—a decline which approached a billion dollars compared to the year-earlier level—was much larger than the accumulation of $280 million in reserves (net of forward runoffs, and excluding the Special Drawing Rights allocation), although the influence of moral suasion in this is unclear because of the easier monetary conditions in Canada.

The easy assumption to make would be that, since moral suasion can have the same effect as market intervention (keeping down the exchange rate without the general stimulative effects which would follow from expansive monetary policies), it should be put in the same category with market intervention, with the same general principles applied as above. But the source of provincial funds raises questions of its own, and once we delve into these complications they throw doubt on the possibility of developing simple rules of thumb to cover exchange fund activities.

The financing of provinces or states is likely to be a source of political concern within federal systems, both because of the great taxing powers of the federal government and because of the relationship between the federal finances and central bank operations. While the Bank of Canada operates in the market for government of Canada bonds, it does not wish to become involved in the purchase of provincial securities, for obvious political (and also legal) reasons.

[5] Even though the responses are very slow in this area, this does not mean that we have a case of "perverse elasticities," because of the use of U.S. dollars in contracts. In an extreme case, if there were no response at all of quantities traded in the short run, and if all contracts were in U.S. dollars, an appreciation would leave the bilateral trade in those items unaffected in size, as measured in U.S. dollars.

The issue applies to more than central bank operations, and the use of funds became a central question in the development of the Canada Pension Plan. The revenue sharing discussion in the United States touches on some of the same issues.

While the Bank of Canada does not directly finance provincial governments, its operations obviously affect the conditions under which the provinces borrow. The proceeds from an open market sale to the Bank of Canada may find their way into provincial government securities. But there is another, and for our purposes very important, link between federal finances and the provinces. Take the case of provincial borrowing in New York. If the Exchange Fund Account purchases the U.S. dollars resulting from the transactions, the account will be indirectly providing the funds for the provinces through the intermediation of the New York capital market—as was noted by Finance Minister Benson:

> When the provinces and municipalities borrow abroad the conversion of the proceeds into Canadian dollars in and of itself exerts upward pressure on the value of the Canadian dollar. If the exchange rate rises this will have economic effects within the region. If the national authorities acquire the proceeds of the borrowing in the exchange market, as may sometimes be the case, they in effect finance the needs of the province and local authorities.[6]

If the Bank of Canada provides the financing for the Exchange Fund Account, the circle is complete, with the central bank having provided financing to the provinces through the intermediation of the New York market and the exchange fund.[7]

Compared to direct purchases of provincial securities by the central bank, this may seem like a complicated way of providing financial resources to the provinces. But the complexity—as well as the loss to Canada from a higher interest rate paid in New York by the provinces than is earned by Canada on her reserves—may be

---

[6] *Proceedings of the Standing Senate Committee on National Finance* (Ottawa), June 29, 1971.

[7] In any particular case, it is unlikely to be clear the degree to which financial needs of the government for exchange fund operations may have influenced the acquisition of government securities by the bank. However, the Bank of Canada (*Annual Report*, 1970, p. 7) notes "the important influence on monetary developments of the fiscal position of the Government and the foreign exchange position. . . . [The central bank] cannot avoid being concerned with the magnitude of the increases in interest rates that would be required to alter substantially the willingness of non-bank investors to hold Government securities."

justified in order to prevent the headaches associated with direct financing.

There is a question as to whether such a roundabout capital flow should be considered as fundamentally an international transaction at all, or whether it should be considered as fundamentally a domestic transaction in which New York just happens to be involved. If the latter position is taken, then there is little objection to be made to exchange fund accumulations of dollars associated with provincial securities issues in New York. This obviously undercuts the general presumption (see the preceding two sections) that countries should confine their reserve acquisitions to periods when their currencies are rising on the exchanges.

Once the door is opened for this exception, a similar question can be raised regarding corporate borrowings in New York. Is it not legitimate for the Canadian government to provide financing to its corporations through the intermediation of the New York market (i.e., acquire U.S. dollars equivalent to corporate borrowings in New York)? Furthermore, does a country have a categorical right to demand that others accept payment in goods and services for past foreign borrowings as they mature? (This implies that reserve accumulation up to the level of total borrowing, and not just net borrowing, is acceptable behavior.) And, if countries have the right to provide the indirect financing for their provinces and corporations through the intermediation of the exchange fund and the New York market (assuming that the United States does not block access to the market), do they not equally have the categorical right to exhort their provinces and corporations to borrow at home rather than abroad, even though this may be intended as a means of keeping down the exchange rate?

Unless one rejects out of hand the concept of the New York market as an intermediary—which I find very difficult to do—the criteria applied to exchange fund operations tend to collapse (with the possible exception of the criterion that countries should avoid sudden, sharp shifts—which is in itself questionable in a world accustomed to adjustable pegs). *The criteria cannot be determined independently of some agreement on the desirable international structure of the balance of payments.*

The special position of the United States. Of the policies which work in part or in whole through the international accounts, increases in tariffs (or, alternatively, quotas) were held in the discussion above to be the most objectionable means for dealing with domestic problems, since a response in kind by other countries would probably leave each country worse off. At the other end of the spectrum, expansive monetary policies which work in part through a repelling of capital and a depreciation of the exchange rate were held to be unobjectionable, since a response in kind would leave the overall expansive domestic effects of the monetary policy. In the intermediate position was placed exchange fund operations: responses in kind by other countries should tend to cancel out the initial intervention, though possibly with bad side effects.

In practice, however, market intervention may create special problems for the United States because of the key position of the U.S. dollar in the international monetary system. If a European country, for example, were to depress its currency by market intervention, and a trading neighbor were to respond with market intervention of its own, the effects on the exchange rate between the two countries might be cancelled out, but both currencies would be depressed with respect to the dollar if the market intervention were to involve the accumulation of dollars. Thus, in a world of generally flexible exchange rates subject to market intervention, other countries might adjust their exchange rates and trade balances to the needs of their domestic economies, with the United States being in the uncomfortable residual position, having whatever trade balance is consistent with the cumulative desires of other countries as expressed in their intervention policies.

This is not a situation confined to flexible rates accompanied by market intervention; it has also been present in the adjustable peg system. Indeed, one of the more interesting paradoxes of the sixties has been that, in spite of the endless talk of a U.S. balance of payments problem, the actual exchange rate decisions of other industrial countries indicated that on average they thought that the U.S. balance of payments was *too strong, and not too weak:* during the sixties, the average exchange rate adjustment for the other industrial countries was a *devaluation* of 0.89 percent with respect to the U.S. dollar.[8] In other words, while there was a general view that the U.S. balance of payments was too weak, this view was not reflected when it came down to the decisions of other countries on their exchange rates. It may, on the other hand, be argued that this system worked to the advantage of the United States, since the use of the dollar as an intervention currency meant that other countries committed themselves to financing our long-term investments and other foreign ex-

[8] International Monetary Fund, *The Role of Exchange Rates in the Adjustment of International Payments,* September 1970, p. 39.

penditures by accumulating liquid dollar assets (or, in the Canadian case, by accumulating nonliquid assets issued by the U.S. Treasury).

The United States has three possible responses to this problem. It can view the advantages of the intervention currency role, and the continuing access to payments financing at generally low rates, as more than compensating for the discomforts of the key currency role: and it will then acquiesce in the residual role.[9] Second, it can take an active role in the exchange market in order to influence exchange rates. Third, it can take direct actions on the current account in order to encourage other countries to negotiate the exchange rate alignments, and in order to move towards a trade balance which it considers satisfactory. The President's August announcement involved a combination of the first and third approaches, with the stress on the third. The suspension of gold payments indicated that potential and actual gold outflows would not in the future be the complicating factor they were in the sixties. The gold suspension and the import surcharge were aimed at encouraging currency revaluations and at improving the trade balance directly.

As a general principle, the passive strategy has considerable appeal, though a case could be made for departing from it in 1971. The case depended on the very rapid shift in the balance of payments, and, in particular, on the very rapid change in the merchandise trade balance from a surplus of $300 million in the first quarter of 1971 to a deficit of $1 billion in the second. The extent and speed of the U.S. deterioration indicated that exchange rate adjustments were in order, even though part of the trade swing could be attributed to special factors, particularly strikes.

The U.S. announcements that it was suspending gold payments and that it expected exchange rates to adjust would in themselves have created upward pressures in the markets for other currencies (compare the Canadian budget declaration of 1961). In the event, of course, the United States went beyond this to preempt bargaining power by imposing the surcharge. The earlier discussion suggests that exchange market intervention would have been a preferable way of increasing pressures on other countries. In practice, however, the ability of the U.S. to engage in direct intervention is circumscribed. Because of the key position of the United States in the monetary system, the tradition has become firmly fixed that the United States

---

[9] See Gottfried Haberler and Thomas Willett, *A Strategy for U.S. Balance of Payments Policy* (Washington: American Enterprise Institute for Public Policy Research, 1971); Lawrence B. Krause, "A Passive Balance of Payments Strategy for the United States," *Brookings Papers on Economic Activity*, 3, 1970, pp. 339-60.

should not intervene in the market for other currencies without the agreement of the country involved. More important, perhaps (since a number of international niceties were in any case going to be violated), was the difficulty of intervening in the market for the currency which seemed most clearly to be out of line. The closeness of Japanese government control over the yen-dollar market complicated any U.S. attempt to force revaluation through exchange market pressures over the resistance of the Japanese government.

A variation on the market pressure theme does, nevertheless, suggest itself: pressures might be increased for foreign revaluations by a dismantling of the U.S. capital controls.[10] The capital controls were instituted when it was considered important to limit foreign holdings of dollars. With the U.S. having openly declared its desire for foreign revaluations, however, increases in foreign dollar holdings would have fitted in with U.S. objectives. The import surcharges, which were a partial substitute for the elimination of capital controls as a means of providing a revaluation incentive, raised problems quite apart from the direct disruptions of trade. These were the dangers that the surcharges might have been very difficult to remove, and that they might after a period have called forth retaliation and an elimination of the postwar trade liberalization. Trade surcharges depress the market value of foreign currencies, and thus make revaluations more difficult. The problem therefore became one of negotiating a simultaneous adjustment of exchange rates and elimination of the import surcharge.

In the longer run, the case for a substantially passive balance of payments position for the United States becomes stronger. It is true that there may be a problem for the United States as the "residual" country under either a pegged exchange rate system or a system of exchange flexibility with intervention by exchange funds: this, along with broader international considerations, underlines the importance of the unresolved problem of internationally acceptable intervention. Nevertheless, the dangers are considerable if the U.S. takes a strongly active balance of payments role. In particular, if the United States returns to trade restrictions when it feels that its products face "unfair" competition, and if other countries take a similar stance, a

[10] In his September 30, 1971, speech to the IMF-IBRD meetings Secretary Connally stated: "While dealing with the monetary system as a whole, we shall, for our part, also proceed with the associated task of dismantling unfair barriers to trade and impediments, including our own, to the free flow of long-term capital." International Monetary Fund, *Summary Proceedings, Annual Meeting*, 1971, p. 221. The deferral of commitments under the capital controls gained some of the advantages which would have come from dismantling the controls.

retreat into protection may result because of the natural disagreement over what constitutes "fair" competition. The sum of "fair shares" has a disconcerting tendency to add to substantially more than 100 percent of the total of world trade.

This danger is emphasized by the tendency for the United States to define fair treatment as that which will allow the United States to rebuild the "healthy" merchandise surplus of the early sixties. Yet it is not clear that equilibrium in future years will involve such a large U.S. merchandise surplus: indeed, it may possibly involve a merchandise deficit. The United States has for years been exporting capital at a sizable rate; earnings from these past investments are growing rapidly (totalling $8.7 billion on private investments in 1970). Unless the United States is to export an ever growing amount of capital—and it is not clear why it should—then equilibrium may come in the future to involve modest deficits on the capital account, on the merchandise trade account, and in military transactions, with these deficits being covered by earnings on foreign investments. If, over an extended period, the United States insists that a sizable trade surplus constitutes the natural state of affairs, and if we enforce this view with trade restrictions whenever we consider them necessary, then we may be in for real trouble. It will be difficult to insist on payments on our past investments unless we allow foreigners to earn the money for the payments.

Logically, a greater degree of exchange flexibility should lessen this danger by encouraging an overall look at the balance of payments. With a fully flexible exchange rate, for instance, the protection of a single product, or of goods in general, does not lead to any (continuing) trade balance improvement, since the exchange rate adjusts in such a manner as to compensate in the form of reduced exports and less depressed imports. Yet the Canadian experience, and, specifically, the policies during 1960, suggest that the logic of the flexible exchange rate is not always understood. Whatever the advantages of exchange flexibility—and they are considerable in monetary and other policy independence—no exchange rate system will be a substitute for an understanding of the interrelation among balance of payments accounts, or for international compromises in the face of disagreements over the nature of payments equilibrium.

7
CONCLUDING REMARKS

It is still too early to evaluate comprehensively the current Canadian experiment with flexible exchange rates. But it is not too early to come to tentative conclusions about the entire Canadian postwar experience. Nor is it entirely fanciful to claim that these conclusions can throw light on the advisability of flexible exchange rates. Indeed, the unique Canadian postwar experience with exchange flexibility makes Canada the obvious source of empirical data on the operation of flexible exchange rates. At the same time, the special features of the Canadian economy—and, in particular, its exceptionally close ties to the predominant U.S. economy—make it inadvisable to apply the Canadian lessons to other countries without a cautious evaluation of their particular circumstances.

One of the more interesting features of the Canadian experience is the way in which the early postwar events foreshadowed similar occurrences in Europe during the 1960s. Between 1945 and 1950, the Canadian government had obvious difficulty in establishing a lasting peg under the International Monetary Fund system. The par value of the currency was raised in 1946, lowered in 1949, and, by mid-1950, the recently chosen par was coming under increasing question. The problem of 1950, when capital inflows complicated the anti-inflationary fight, has a parallel in the difficulties which Germany faced in 1961, 1969, and 1971. The problem arose earlier for Canada because of its particularly close connection with the U.S. capital market.

During the early part of the float, and especially between 1950 and 1952, exchange flexibility demonstrated its usefulness in insulating the Canadian economy from external disturbances. A simple upward adjustment of the peg in 1950 would, of course, have provided some of the advantages of the float. But, while the strength of the capital account was clear in 1950, the strong current account performance of 1951-52 could not be foreseen at the time when the currency was released from its peg. Thus, an upward revaluation of the Canadian dollar could have provided a degree of insulation from the domestic effects of the 1950 capital account surplus, but it is not reasonable to assume that the Canadian government in 1950 could have chosen a sufficient revaluation to compensate for the 1951-52 strength in the current account. And herein lay the beauty of the flexible exchange rate: market forces operating on the exchange rate provided an automatic adjustment to the unforeseen strength in the balance of payments.

In the later part of the flexible exchange rate period, 1958-62, the experience was much less happy. In this period, the major changes in the exchange rate were not primarily a reflection of external balance of payments forces. Rather, they reflected the strong anti-inflationary policies of the Bank of Canada, which pushed up interest rates, attracted capital, and contributed to a weak performance on merchandise account. Two strong lessons stand out from this experience. Exchange rate flexibility can significantly add to the power of monetary policy. And it is therefore particularly important that monetary policy be in line with the needs of the domestic economy. Unfortunately, the policies of the Bank of Canada did not meet this standard between 1958 and 1961: monetary conditions were much too tight in the face of high levels of unemployment and reasonably stable domestic price levels.

During the 1962-70 period of a pegged rate, the most interesting feature of the Canadian experience was the relationship between U.S. balance of payments programs and Canadian domestic stabilization policies. In theory, the fixed exchange rate, and the commitments which Canada made to keep her reserves below a ceiling, could have severely restricted the freedom of action of Canadian monetary policy. In practice, this restriction was not very severe, at least not until 1970. In part, this was due to the compromises worked out between the U.S. and Canadian governments over the balance of payments programs; in part, it was due to the lack of desire by the Canadian authorities to initiate policies which would have greatly altered reserve holdings.

In 1970, when the decision was made to allow the Canadian dollar to float again, the domestic needs of the Canadian economy were much less sharply defined than had been the case at the time of the 1950 float. This was not a period of excess demand, when restraint was clearly called for. Nor was it a repeat of 1958-61 when the Canadian economy required (but did not get) expansive monetary policies. Rather, the 1970 economy presented a dilemma, with unemployment and inflation both constituting difficult problems. Exchange flexibility was chosen as a way of balancing conflicting considerations. The upward movement of the currency on the exchanges was seen as necessary to avoid the drastically easier monetary conditions which would have defeated the price stability objective. At the same time, moderate expansive steps were taken to offset the restrictive effects of the currency appreciation.

While the exchange appreciation and domestic policies were thus designed to partially balance one another in terms of their overall aggregate demand, there is some reason to believe that the combined policies somewhat reduced the unemployment-inflation dilemma. This is because exchange appreciation has two restraining effects on price levels—that working through aggregate demand, and the direct effects of the appreciation on the prices of imports and exports. Thus, when the effects of the appreciation on aggregate demand are accompanied by expansive domestic policies, it should be possible to get a better price performance with no worse performance on the employment front, or a better employment performance with no greater increase in prices.

While there is some evidence that the appreciation did indeed soften the unemployment-price dilemma, there is insufficient evidence to come to any categorical conclusion. Nevertheless, a very important lesson is involved. Depreciations or restrictions on imports may make the unemployment situation worse, not better. Since these steps tend to increase prices directly, they may induce policy makers to adopt more restrictive monetary policies, more than offsetting the direct employment effects of the depreciation or import restriction. Depreciations and tariffs make the price-unemployment dilemma worse; they are, in effect, negative "incomes policies."

Cover and book design: Pat Taylor